AMERICAN BUSINESS ABROAD

Origins and Development
of the Multinational Corporation

This is a volume in the Arno Press collection

AMERICAN BUSINESS ABROAD

Origins and Development
of the Multinational Corporation

Advisory Editor
STUART BRUCHEY

Associate Editor
ELEANOR BRUCHEY

Editorial Board
RAYMOND VERNON
MIRA WILKINS

*See last pages of this volume for
a complete list of titles*

The American Invaders

F[red] A. McKenzie

ARNO PRESS
A New York Times Company
1976

Editorial Supervision: SHEILA MEHLMAN

———◆———

Reprint Edition 1976 by Arno Press Inc.

Reprinted from a copy in
  The University of Illinois Library

AMERICAN BUSINESS ABROAD: Origins and
Development of the Multinational Corporation
ISBN for complete set: 0-405-09261-X
See last pages of this volume for titles.

Manufactured in the United States of America

———◆———

Library of Congress Cataloging in Publication Data

Mackenzie, Frederick Arthur, 1869-1931.
    The American invaders.

    (American business abroad)
    Reprint of the 1902 ed. published by G. Richards,
London.
    1. United States--Commerce--History.
2. Investments, American--History. 3. United
States--Foreign economic relations. I. Title.
II. Series.
HF3029.M32 1976   338.91'41'073   76-5016
ISBN 0-405-09284-9

THE AMERICAN INVADERS

The American Invaders

BY

F. A. McKENZIE

Have the elder races halted?
Do they droop and end their lesson, wearied
over there beyond the seas?
We take up the task eternal, and the burden
and the lesson,
Pioneers! O Pioneers!
—WALT WHITMAN.

London
Grant Richards
1902

BUTLER & TANNER,
THE SELWOOD PRINTING WORKS,
FROME, AND LONDON.

CONTENTS

" THE war, I fear, is the war of trade which is unmistakably upon us. When I look round me I cannot blind my eyes to the fact that so far as we can predict anything of the twentieth century on which we have now entered, it is that it will be one of acutest international conflict in point of trade. We were the first nation in the world—of the modern world—to discover that trade was an absolute necessity. For that we were nick-named a nation of shop-keepers. But now every nation wishes to be a nation of shop-keepers too; and when we look at the character of some of these nations, and when we look at the in-telligence of their preparations, we may well feel that it behoves us not to fear, but to gird up our loins in preparation for what is before us. There are two nations which are obviously our rivals and opponents in this commercial warfare that is to come. To America and to Germany we have to look in the future for an acute and increasing competition in regard to our trade, and I am bound to say that in looking at these two countries there is much to apprehend. The alertness of the Americans, their incalculable natural resources, their acuteness, their enterprise, their vast population, which will in all proba-bility within the next twenty years reach 100,000,000, make them very formidable competitors with ourselves."

LORD ROSEBERY, Jan. 16, 1901.

PREFACE

IT has been my endeavour in this book neither to minimize nor exaggerate the industrial triumphs of America. I have counted it no business of mine unduly to depreciate British manufacturers or to gloss over their successes. So far as I could learn the facts, whether for or against the Americans, I have recorded them. In some parts the views here expressed sharply differ from those of many recognized experts on the particular trades dealt with. Where such differences come they have not been made without careful consideration of the facts supporting the other side.

It is no longer necessary to insist on the supreme importance to our trade of the issues here raised. Opinions about the need of industrial reform, which a year ago one dared only state with almost bated breath, are now the commonplaces of the man in the street. We move rapidly in these days, and the entire self-confidence of our industrial supremacy which held the minds of most Englishmen not long since has now given way to a perhaps undue sense of depression. The American invasion of Europe is no longer a matter of abstract discussion. It has touched Europe at a hundred points, and has affected no country so largely as our own.

Although the trend of many of the facts in the following pages is of necessity pessimistic, I would protect myself against being supposed to believe that the day of English trade prosperity has finally passed. Undoubtedly our commerce has received a check. We slept while our rivals went ahead. We have been too content to rest satisfied with the great accomplishments of past generations. We have been a little too prosperous, and far too easy going. For this, masters and men must share the blame alike. Are we, then, to conclude that our nation is from now to be regarded as a negligible factor in this world's story ? Are we to believe, as some superficial observers proclaim, that while England has played her part—a grand enough part in her time— henceforth she is to be reckoned as a decaying and declining force ? If this were true it would be a bad thing, not only for England, but for all who have dealings with her. Happily it is not true. Those who know anything of the great reserve strength of this Empire are best aware that our nation need only rouse herself in earnest to recover much lost ground. In spite of certain prominent shortcomings, there is yet a stubbornness, a persistency, a straightforwardness of dealing and famous honesty of manufacture among English traders to which the world can show no equal. English goods still have a name in many lands of being the best. A great, though unhappily diminishing prestige is behind us, enormous wealth lies in our hands, and our people were never more intelligent. The future still waits for us if we will to have it. But to hold our own there must be reform far reaching and thorough. It is to help to bring needed changes that this book is written.

CHAPTER I

THE EXPANSION OF AMERICA

" In the four quarters of the globe, who reads an American book ? or goes to an American play ? or looks at an American picture or statue ? What does the world yet owe to American physicians or surgeons ? What new substances have their chemists discovered ? or what old ones have they analyzed ? What new constellations have been discovered by the telescopes of Americans ? What have they done in the mathematics ? Who drinks out of American glasses ? or eats from American plates ? or wears American coats or gowns ? or sleeps in American blankets ?"
—SYDNEY SMITH.

AMERICA has invaded Europe not with armed men, but with manufactured products. Its leaders have been captains of industry and skilled financiers, whose conquests are having a profound effect on the every-day lives of the masses from Madrid to St. Petersburg.

No nation has felt the results of this invasion more than England. Our one speech, our common ways of life, and the large reserve wealth of our traders, naturally made ours a favourite vantage ground for the Americans in starting their Eastern campaigns. Men have sometimes spoken as though the dramatic *coup* of a Morgan, when he took our Atlantic supremacy from us ; of a Schwab, who outbids our steel makers ; of Philadelphian bridge builders, who capture the orders for our biggest viaducts, comprise this invasion. They form but a very small part of it. Such items are merely the sensational incidents in a vast campaign. The real invasion goes on unceasingly and with little noise or fuss in five hundred industries at once. From shaving soap to electric motors, and from tools to telephones, the American is clearing the field.

Ten years ago England was easily first in the iron, shipping, cotton, and coal industries. We took from America raw food products in considerable quantities, but America was our greatest customer for manufactured goods. Now the situation is changed, and changed with a suddenness which makes the transformation the more vivid. We have lost our supremacy in coal output, and even our export fuel trade is being hotly attacked. In the production of iron and steel we are far outstripped. In cotton we are declining, while America is rapidly expanding. In shipping the ownership of some of our greatest lines has been acquired by American companies : the Atlantic freight trade, where we were once almost alone, has gone in fact, if not in name, from us, and our position in the Pacific is threatened. Still more significant is it that the organization of most of the great schemes proposed on novel lines for England to-day are in American hands and the fruit of American brains.

Where not long since America was our largest customer, we are now the largest and most profitable buyers from America. One-third of the total imports that enter this country come from the United States, and for every £1 America pays us for commercial products we pay America £3 15s. This of course is a process that cannot go on indefinitely, save by the absorption by Americans of the profits we make from other lands. If there were no other factors in our international trade but these, such unequal exchange would of necessity in due time land us in insolvency. There are, needless to say, many other factors. But the ill-balanced trading has resulted in a considerable transference of British wealth to America. To-day we float large portions of our national loans in New York, and the taxpayers of this country yield revenue to the American holders of our bonds. Ten years ago we held the bonds and the Americans paid us the interest.

The preliminary reports of the census of the United States for 1900, given on the next page, show in most effective form the industrial expansion of the land for thirty years past.

And this expansion is only at its commencement. It will receive its set-backs and will have temporary checks. The present boom may be followed quicker than many expect by a time of real industrial ferment and of financial strain. The artificial inflation of securities which has marked the way of American finance recently is bound to cause some trouble. But checks and set-backs can do little more than cause momentary delay. America is bound to ad-

COMPARATIVE SUMMARY, WITH PER CENT. OF INCREASE FOR LAST DECADE.

	a 1900.	Date of Census.			Inc. p.c. 1890 to 1900.
		1890.	1880.	1870.	
Number of establishments	512,726	355,415	253,852	252,148	44·3
Capital	$9,874,664,087	$6,525,156,486	$2,790,272,606	$2,118,208,769	51·3
Salaried officials, clerks, etc., No.	397,730	b 461,009	c...	c...	d 13·7
Salaries	$404,837,591	b $391,988,208	c...	c...	3·3
Wage-earners, average number	5,321,087	4,251,613	2,732,595	2,053,996	25·2
Total wages	$2,330,273,021	$1,891,228,321	$947,953,795	$775,584,343	23·2
Men, 16 years and over	4,120,716	3,327,042	2,019,035	1,615,598	23·9
Wages	$2,022,899,275	$1,659,234,483	c...	c...	21·9
Women, 16 years and over	1,031,747	803,686	531,639	323,770	28·4
Wages	$281,705,586	$215,367,976	c...	c...	30·8
Children, under 16 years	168,624	120,885	181,921	114,628	39·5
Wages	$25,668,160	$16,625,862	c...	c...	54·4
Miscellaneous expenses	$1,028,855,586	$631,225,035	e...	e...	63·0
Cost of materials used	$7,360,954,597	$5,162,044,076	$3,396,823,549	$2,488,427,242	42·6
Value of products, including custom work and repairing	$13,040,013,638	$9,372,437,283	$5,369,579,191	$4,232,325,442	39·1

a Includes, for comparative purposes, 85 governmental establishments in the District of Columbia having products valued at $9,887,355, the statistics of such establishments for 1890 not being separable. b Includes proprietors and firm members, with their salaries; number only reported in 1900. c Not reported separately. d Decrease. e Not reported.

vance, and never will her manufacturing facilities be more formidable in competition for the trade of the world than in the days of falling prices and commercial trouble.

The shifting of the financial control of the world from London to New York is not an affair which can be described by exact statistics, but that it is steadily going on few familiar with international money affairs will deny. The daily operations of the New York Exchange, as Mr. Carnegie points out, exceed those of London. The banking resources of the United States are about twice those of Great Britain. The expansion of American trade has prepared the field for American bankers, and now, late in the day, American capital is being launched in bulk in the establishment of trading banks abroad.

The founding of the International Banking Corporation, with a capital of $12,000,000, early this year in New York City, is one sign of activity here. This corporation, which largely owes its start to the Equitable Life Assurance Society, has on its list of directors twenty-three of the most solid names in the American business world, including Mr. Harriman, chairman of the Union Pacific Railroad; Mr. Edwin Gould; Mr. Abram S. Hewitt; Mr. H. E. Huntington; Mr. Frick, of the Steel Trust; and Mr. Delano, of Brown, Shipley and Co. These names are sufficient proof that the new corporation can obtain all the money it wants. Its purpose is quite frankly stated. It intends to fight for a share in the banking trade of the Far East, a part of the world once our own banking preserve. It has opened its branch in London, it is establishing branches in the great trading centres of the East, and is already securing substantial business. It is part of the rapidly maturing American scheme for the capture of the Pacific.

What the International Banking Corporation is doing other Americans are also attempting. The American financier is more accessible and more open to business than his older European rival. He lends on character, and takes business risks which Lombard Street would instantly reject. This is why, with initiative and daring, American financiers are stepping into the very heart of our own businesses. It is a recognized fact in finance to-day that if capital is required for any great English scheme, particularly if it has to do with electric traction, it is simpler and easier to get it from America than England.

Both in exports and imports England is far and away America's largest customer. Of every dollar received by America for foreign trade last year fifty-three cents came from the British Empire. Of these fifty-three cents the United Kingdom alone paid forty cents. Of every dollar America paid abroad for trade the British Empire received thirty-one cents, and England alone seventeen cents. The whole British Empire pays the United States nearly three dollars for every dollar America pays it in way of trade ; and for every four dollars America paid the United Kingdom alone, in the same way we paid it fifteen dollars. To avoid overburdening this chapter with statistics I have placed the exact figures at the end.

The tendency, apart from exceptional years, is for the American imports rapidly to increase. In two years the increase in their value to England has been £18,000,000.

Of what do these imports consist ? It would be easier to say what they do not include. Certain lines of them are a direct source of wealth to us. American food, which arrives in enormous quantities, is welcomed by all now that we are no longer an agricultural nation. American raw products, such as pig iron, are further sources of wealth. But a very large part of the imports consists of manufactured goods in lines which were once produced here. Of these boots are a notable instance, and in Northampton workmen are on short time to-day and children have gone hungry to school during the winter because part of our shoe trade has been taken from us.

Sheffield, long leader in the tool world, now gets its newest machine tools from Pennsylvania—as Paris, long dominant mistress of fashion, now takes many of its styles from New York.

In London the American invasion shows itself on every side. Morgan fights Yerkes for the right to build our tubes. American capital is transforming our dirty and suffocating " undergrounds " to the brightness and cleanness of electricity. The theatrical trust has its grip over many of our theatres and over a number of our best actors. The English branch of the Oil Trust dictates the price of our petroleum and supplies us with it. The Beef Trust of Chicago regulates the prices and supplies of our meat, and grain dealers in the same city control the price of our bread. Our aristocracy marry American wives, and their coachmen are giving place to American-trained drivers of American-built automobiles. American novels are filling our library shelves, and American schemes of book distribution are revolutionizing our old ways. Parcels delivery carts may soon give place to a gigantic American pneumatic tube service, now in process of organization. Whole districts in the centre of London are passing into the hands of American landlords.

Our chemists' shops are full of Transatlantic drugs. Our bootmakers devote their windows to the finest manufactures from Boston, while our leading shopkeepers go across the Atlantic to learn the art of window dressing. For months at a time the stars and stripes float from many of the largest buildings off Trafalgar Square. Some of our hotels are more American than if they were on Broadway, and Bloomsbury from April to October is an American colony. Our very jokes are machine-made in the offices of New York publishers, for almost every English " comic " paper of the cheaper sort gets its humour, so called, week by week, by columns of clippings from journals on the other side. Our babies are fed on American foods, and our dead buried in American coffins.

To-day it is literally true that Americans are selling their cottons in Manchester and their steel tools in Sheffield. A few months since they were sending their pig iron to Lancashire, and soon they will be doing it again. They send oatmeal to Scot-

land and our national beef to England. It only remains for them to take coals to Newcastle. In fact
the time seems coming when, as an American wittily
put it, we shall find our chief export across the
Atlantic to be scions of our nobility, whom America
cannot produce on account of the limits imposed by
her constitution. And there the balance of trade
will be in our favour, even though America sends us
her gracious daughters to grace our ducal homes.

" There are hatfuls of gold waiting to be gathered
up in London," said a returning Yankee plutocrat
to a Chicago reporter not long since. Our fathers
went West to make their fortunes ; their sons are
coming East to do the same. The word has gone
forth from East to West that here in England men
with brains and energy can make more and under
easier conditions than in America. Hence the rush
of men and goods East, a rush which cannot wholly
be shown in statistical form, but which touches our
trade on every side.

On the Continent of Europe the invasion, although
less serious than with us, has produced greater alarm.
The facts have been so ably summarized in the
official *Review of the World's Commerce*, issued by
the U.S. Government, that I am tempted to make
a somewhat lengthy quotation :—

" Austria-Hungary (is) the country in which
originated the idea of European combination against
American goods, and where the hostility of the
industrial forces continues to be most pronounced.
Notwithstanding this the imports from the United
States, according to Consul-General Hurst of Vienna,

are increasing rapidly, although American exporters have not until recently given general attention to that part of Europe, 'which is considerably removed from ports in closest touch with
Transatlantic commerce.' So formidable is the
growth of American imports in fact that 'Austrian
manufacturers and agriculturists are making an
organized effort to stem the inflow.' At a recent
conference in Vienna to take measures against
American competition, adds Mr. Hurst, 'it was
openly acknowledged that the commercial policy
of the present time is dictated and controlled by
the United States. . . . Instances of the gigantic
strides of our American manufacturing industries
are cited to show our capability to forge ahead
of all competitors in many fields.'

" In a report upon the commerce and industries of
Germany, Consul-General Mason, of Berlin, says the
United States again heads the list of countries selling
to that country, with a total of nearly $243,000,000,
or 16·9 per cent. of the entire bulk of German imports, although it should be noted that this covers
the values of all American products landed on
German soil, 'a large percentage of which simply
pass through . . . en route to Russia, Austria-
Hungary, Switzerland, and Scandinavia.' It may
be expected that later returns will show a falling off
in German imports, owing to the recent industrial
depression which has seriously impaired the purchasing power of the Empire. But in Germany, as
in Austria-Hungary, our goods continue to hold their
own, and the 'overshadowing competition of the

United States' is regarded by German economists
as of grave importance to the future of German
industry and commerce. ' It is recognized by intelligent Germans,' adds Mr. Mason, ' that in future
industrial and trade competitions, that fine com-
posite product of American racial qualities, institu-
tions and methods, the working man who thinks
will, in combination with our unequalled resources,
turn the scale in favour of the United States.'

" The same concern is felt in France, in Belgium,
in Switzerland, in Great Britain—in other words,
in all of the highly-developed manufacturing countries of Europe, and it is a most significant fact that,
even in specialties which were once thought to be
exclusively their own, the United States is becoming
a more and more formidable competitor. Who
would have imagined a few years ago that we would
make such rapid progress in the manufacture of silk
that we would soon cease buying silks from France,
with the exception of highly-finished goods, and
would actually be exporting silks to that country ?
Yet this is what has happened. So of tin plate in
Wales. At one time it was doubtful whether we
could manufacture tin plate profitably, and it was
confidently asserted that the Welsh must always
control the American trade. But we now manufacture all the tin plate we need, and the Welsh have
recently imported tin bars from us.

"There are, indeed, surprisingly few of the articles
which used to be obtained exclusively abroad that
are not now produced in the United States. The
woollen as well as the silk industry of France and the

hosiery industry of Germany are said to be suffering severely from our competition, and the Bohemian glass industry is feeling the effect of the increase of glass manufacture in the United States.   Our cottons are steadily gaining in taste and finish, and are now sold in England in competition with the Manchester product.

" Says the *Leipziger Tageblatt* of April 10, 1901 :— ' Even in fancy articles, in which the European market has set the styles for the entire world, the American manufacturers are beginning to compete with the European.   British calico prints are already receiving competition from America.   We hear that travellers of a well-known American house have offered American cotton stuffs in England with much success, and the London authorities declare them to be tasteful and worth their price.'

" A New York company manufacturing cotton stuffs intends to found a Paris house which shall introduce its fancy woven stuffs for women's dresses, and trimmed women's hats are being exported from the United States to Europe.   ' The reversible cloths which are made in the United States,' said Consul Sawter of Glauchau, in a report sent in 1900, ' are now the style in high-priced goods in the German capital.'

" In agriculture, as in manufactures, we are constantly widening the sphere of our production.   The orange and lemon growers of southern Europe are feeling the effect of California's competition.   ' It is ridiculous,' exclaims a Spanish newspaper, ' to think that fruits and vegetables raised on the slopes of the

distant Pacific should compete at the very doors of
Spain with those produced in this country. . . .
Shall we live to see American oranges on the Valencia
market itself ? ' We are producing our own raisins,
our prunes, our wines, our olive oil, and are sending
them abroad. California prunes now compete in
Europe with Bosnian prunes, once a staple article
of export to New York.

"In the busy manufacturing district of Liege,
Belgium, according to the annual report of Consul
Winslow, more American goods are consumed than
ever before, in spite of business depression. 'Our
sales, in general,' says Mr. Winslow, ' have doubled
in the past three years, and it is now common to see
articles marked " Americaine " in the shop windows.'
Spanish journals complain that steel rails are imported from the United States, notwithstanding the
production of iron is one of the important industries
of Spain. Vice-Consul Wood of Madrid says our
goods are to be seen everywhere."

The exact statistics of American foreign commerce as
given in the advance sheets on imports and exports for
December, 1901, issued by the Treasury Department at
Washington may be of value. They show that for the year
ending December, 1901, out of a total of $1,465,380,919
exports the United Kingdom took $598,766,799 ; British
North America $109,598,695 ; British Australasia took
$30,569,814 ; and the total British Empire took
$784,289,681.

Turning to imports, out of a total of $880,421,056 the
United Kingdom sent $155,291,927 ; British North
America $45,897,256 ; British East Indies $47,171,558 ;
and the total British Empire $273,956,187.

CHAPTER II

THE PLAN OF CAMPAIGN

WHAT are the means the Americans have adopted in their commercial war against Europe ?

Their weapons have been not one, but many. First among them comes the securing of financial control, and the elimination of competition, as far as possible. The American trusts have centralized American forces, and so enabled the blows against us to be directed with greater force and effect.

One main factor in the European war has been the Standard Oil combine, for the oil magnates, parents of the modern trust system, have accumulated such enormous capital in their own hands that they have made themselves, for real power, veritable kings among men.

The Rockefeller group of millionaires was the first to carry to its logical conclusion the altogether sound principle that by combination the producers of one article can obtain greater profits for themselves without adding to the burden of the public. By extending the area of their operations, by at first

14

securing rebates from railway companies, by capturing the great pipe lines, they obtained control,
though not a monopoly, of the oil market of two-
thirds of the world. Their profits have been very
great, although it is impossible to give reliable
figures. The trust officials—for the Standard Oil is
of course a trust in spite of the nominal dissolution of
the trust in answer to legal orders—cleverly disguise
their gains, for they have a not unnatural idea that
this is no business of the outside world. The mere
dividends, high as they are (between thirty and forty
per cent.) do not represent the total profits, for it
has always been a principle of the corporation to
keep back enormous sums and use them in all
manner of developments. Most great trusts are
held by many. This trust is in the hands of few,
the overwhelming proportion of Standard Oil stock
being centralized. Three dozen names cover the
total of the great owners, and the real power and
command practically rests with half a dozen men.
With profits of tens of millions a year the Standard
Oil group has long since ceased to be solely concerned with oil. It has become a great railroad
owner ; it has stretched out beyond the seas ; it
has been the real mover in the conquest of the
Atlantic ; it has entered into banking on a large
scale. The Standard Oil corporation is the Old
Guard of the American invasion, and it is all the
stronger because it moves secretly.

Working with the Standard Oil, sometimes together, sometimes apart, have been other groups,
some making great gains from street traction and

electric power, some from steel, some manufacturers of finished goods. They have heaped up spare capital such as has never in the history of the world been in the hands of a few men before. Behind them has been the savings of the American people, savings of years of plenty. The money power is the great American weapon. While this country is to-day groaning under rapidly-increasing taxes, and while our Exchequer shows a deficit of over a million pounds a week, America is able to remit its special war taxation and is suffering from an over-gorged Treasury.

The spare capital is in the hands of men who know how to use it. The Americans come over here with business notions that make some of our slower-going folk stand aghast. They are quicker and more ready to change than we are. Let me give a typical case, told me by the man who gave the order. Early this year a big West End business house wished to have its premises reconstructed. It consulted a London contractor, who offered to do the work in fourteen months. Then it approached an American builder who has recently set up in this country. He agreed to get the whole thing completed before the Coronation. The American got the contract.

Not long since a short cable tramway was lying un-used on a hill to the north of London. It had had an unfortunate history, and for long could find no pur-chaser. The County Council offered a " scrap-iron " price for the concern, and as there seemed to be no competitors in the field it reckoned it had a real bargain. But just before it completed the deal a quiet American stepped in, outbid the Council, and secured the line at a fractional part of the original cost. He at once set it working. And if you should wish to see how it pays him, go up on a summer's afternoon to Highgate Hill and notice the crowd on the cable cars there.

Last summer the most striking instance of all the triumphs of American machinery was witnessed in London. Bryant and May had long been looked upon as a great English institution, as secure in its place as the Bank of England. It had practically destroyed all serious English competition : it paid dividends of twenty per cent., and its fame was world-wide.

While this house was resting on its reputation and priding itself on its power, an American manufacturer studied the match business. He experimented, employed several smart men in improving old match-making machinery, and spent quite £10,000 a year in developing new apparatus. He sent agents over the world, and wherever a new improvement in match-making machinery was to be had he bought it.

Six years ago this American—Mr. Barber—came over to Liverpool and opened works there. He could turn out matches so much cheaper and so much better than the English makers that Bryant and May suddenly awoke to the fact that they had met a dangerous rival. Bryant and May now looked over the world for new machines, but they found they had been preceded everywhere. Their dividends declined from twenty to fourteen per cent.,

c

and they saw that if things went on all dividends would disappear. Then the American stepped up. He told the managers of the English business that he could beat them out of the field, and they knew that he spoke the truth. But, said he, if Bryant and May would consent to surrender their factories and to give up absolutely all control in the management of the match trade he would take over their shares and guarantee them interest on the fourteen per cent. basis. Bryant and May could do nothing but submit, and their works have now passed into American hands. They could not obtain the best machinery, for the rights in all the improved machinery were owned by the Americans, and so they were beaten.

Mr. Barber, the President of the American and Liverpool Diamond Match Companies, the clever American who accomplished this, frankly told Bryant and May's shareholders how he had been able to do it. " The machinery now being used in Bryant and May's factory," he said, " was the invention of men who had been in the employ of the Diamond company since its inception, but that machinery was discarded by the American company fifteen or sixteen years ago, and we have been gradually improving upon it. I do not think there has been a year when the Diamond company of America has not expended at least 50,000 dollars in experiments in improving their machinery. We have good inventive talent, and we have quite a large number of people working continuously with the sole object of improving our machinery. Then again we have representatives always travelling in different parts of the world for the purpose of acquiring any new invention which would be of assistance to our business. In the purchase of patents we have spent in the last year over 250,000 dollars, and in the last twenty years a million. In five years we have succeeded in building up a trade in the United Kingdom equal in quality to that of Bryant and May, and at the same time we have been able to pay interest on every dollar of capital that has gone into the business. Your board has managed the company as well as the facilities which they possess allow them to do, but they did not improve their machinery, for the reason that they have not a ruling genius among them."

The net result is that the entire match industry of England has passed into American hands.

The management of the trust officially estimated the value of this deal to themselves at over a million dollars, for, as was pointed out to the American shareholders, " All the benefits of this combination inure to the Diamond Match Company, as the Bryant and May Company receive as its share of the future profits the same amount per annum that they earned in 1900, which was the lowest per cent. they had made on their property for many years." And Mr. Barber and his associates are not satisfied with this. From England they are now acquiring Europe. At this time they are busy buying works or establishing factories in Germany, in Switzerland, in the Philippines, and in Chile. They have factories in operation in South Africa and Peru, and for the year 1901 they made an actual profit, excluding the possible great gains over the British deal, of about $2,000,000. They bid fair to create a great match trust which shall include the whole of the Western and much of the Eastern world.

And so the story runs on. While we are pluming ourselves on our own commercial astuteness the Americans are stepping in to the centre of our industrial capital, and are taking from under our eyes the most profitable and the easiest speculations. And, unhampered by restrictive conditions, their workmen turn out goods with which our own cannot attempt to compete.

But the main weapon in the hands of the American invaders is yet to be used. Eleven years ago America practically destroyed our import manufacturing trade to her by creating a high tariff. The protected American manufacturers were able to pull themselves together and to secure higher prices owing to the practical penalizing of our goods. Now American-manufactured goods are able to stand on their own merits, for America can produce at less cost than we can. But the heads of the Republican party, in other words the great manufacturers, have no intention of throwing away the commercial weapon which this high tariff has given them. They will go in, not for free trade, but for reciprocal trade advantages. They will auction tariff concessions for tariff favours, and before many years our manufacturers will find that American dealers have secured special customs and rebates in many lands ; for the American business man believes in getting all the advantages he can. The United States Government holds trade to be worth studying and worth building up, and the trader as the great man. Reciprocity will be the key-note of American politics to-morrow, as protection was yesterday.

The assassination of President McKinley has for the time dealt reciprocity a severe blow. In his speech at Buffalo on September 5, 1901, he, formerly the high priest of Protection, declared for a revolution in the American tariff.

" Our capacity to produce," said he, " has developed so enormously, and our products have so multiplied, that the problem of more markets requires urgent and immediate attention. Only a broad and enlightened policy will keep what we have. By sensible trade arrangements which do not interrupt our home production we shall extend the outlets for our increasing surplus. We must not repose in the fancied security that we can for ever sell everything and buy little or nothing. We should take from our customers such of their products as we can use without harm to our industries and labour.

" Reciprocity is the natural outgrowth of our wonderful industrial development under the domestic policy now firmly established. What we produce beyond our domestic consumption we should send abroad. The period of exclusiveness is past. The expansion of our trade and commerce is a pressing problem. Commercial wars are unprofitable, and reciprocity treaties are in harmony with the spirit of the times, while measures of retaliation are not."

Mr. Kasson, the sometime Special Commissioner representing the United States in the making of treaties for reciprocal trade, took strongly the same line, and in November, 1901, an important conference was held by the American manufacturers on this matter—a conference, however, which was singularly barren of results. Some had hoped that President Roosevelt, himself a free trader when a young man, would specially favour the idea, but the President's declaration on the matter in his message to Congress in December, 1901, was disappointing. " Reciprocity," said he, " must be treated as the handmaiden of protection. Our first duty is to see that the protection granted by a tariff in every case where it is needed is maintained, and that reciprocity be sought for so far as it can safely be done without injuring our home industries. Just how far this is must be determined according to the individual case, remembering always that every application of our tariff policy to meet our shifting national needs must be conditioned upon the cardinal fact that the duties must never be reduced below the point that will cover the difference between the labour here and abroad. The well-being of the wage worker is a prime consideration of our entire policy of economic legislation."

One other thing must not be forgotten. The American business man works harder and works longer than his average English competitor. This is true of almost every grade in the industrial army. Here in England when a man has made a respectable competency he, as a rule, rests on his oars and thinks

prosperity an excuse for ease. The American business man, on the contrary, works harder the higher
he rises ; and though you may find the wives and
daughters of the great Transatlantic industrial kings
spending their days in leisured ease, you find the
kings themselves, as a rule, with a long-distance
telephone at their ears and a couple of stenographers
at their elbows. The head of an English business
thinks he does well if he reaches his office by ten in
the morning : the American is before his desk at
eight. The English workman limits his output : the
American prides himself on working his machines
to their utmost capacity. The difference this makes
may be shown by one case in point. An American
contractor undertook, a year or two since, to erect
a building in London. He found that his English
bricklayers would not lay more than a limited number of bricks each per day. It was not a question of
pay, for he was willing to pay them according to
their work. In despair the contractor brought over
a number of men from New York. He paid them
higher wages, but they worked so much harder than
the Englishmen that, after allowing for the cost of
their passage and return, the contractor materially
saved on the deal. And, what was more important
for him, he was able to complete his work in time.

" Driving " is the rule in American industry. The
foreman or " ganger " there is not a sort of caretaker
of the workman's interest, but a watchman for the
master's. He sees, as it is his business to see, that
every man is kept at the utmost point of exertion
during the whole of his working hours. Admittedly

there are many evil sides to " driving." It means
that the weaklings go to the wall, that the indifferent
workers are ruthlessly thrown on one side, that the
delicate are crushed, and that right quickly. It
means hard times for the strong, and no mercy for
the weak. But between the " driving " of an American steel mill and the happy-go-lucky methods of
an old-fashioned London office there are intermediate
stages.

Already " driving " is coming into London from
sheer industrial necessity, and it must come in more
and more if we are to hold our own. I recently saw
the bad effects of this in a great London warehouse.
There, while the hands are well treated, they work
at such pressure that the name of their firm has
become almost a byword in the city. The results are
very apparent. The house in question continually
drafts in a large number of lads from the country,
and almost as steadily there go back men of broken
health, with seeds of consumption sown in them,
with ruined constitutions—all brought on through
the persistent overwork there maintained. No man
of common sense would advocate this. But English
masters must find a *via media* between indifferent
workmanship and cruel overwork. On their finding
this depends very largely our commercial future.

CHAPTER III

THE FIGHT FOR THE ATLANTIC

MEN have almost forgotten that eight years ago
America seemed on the verge of a great industrial
upheaval. Business was exceedingly bad ; stocks
and shares of all kinds had fallen to their lowest ;
railway after railway was threatened with ruin ;
Coxey and his army of reformers were marching
towards Washington ; the bituminous coal trade,
after a bitter labour fight, had patched up a temporary peace ; Chicago was going through civil war ;
the Pullman strike was on ; the main railway systems of the mid-West were locked up ; the terrible
Homestead struggle was progressing, and the land
rang with the voices of homeless and hungry men.
It was the time when the farmers of the West piled
up their mortgages, and when the toilers of the
Eastern cities found their work brought to an end.

What, it may be asked, has that to do with the
American fight for our Atlantic trade ? Much every
way. It was the industrial trouble of the early
nineties that paved the way to power for Mr. Pierpont Morgan and gave him his grip on the railroad
systems of America.

Mr. Pierpont Morgan was then best known as a leading Anglo-American banker who represented a large portion of the British holders of American securities. In this capacity he had much to do with American railroads. He took up line after line and reorganized it. By supreme business skill he made bankrupt properties solvent. Soon it was found that the interests of various roads were largely identical. Having the power of the purse, he made railroad presidents conform to business principles. Heads of lines who had been indulging in long and costly rate wars at their stockholders' expense were bidden mend their ways.

As times improved and the era of prosperity set in, Mr. Morgan found himself the over-lord of a central group of American railways. The various lines directly under his own hands were about 12,000 miles in extent. In conjunction with Mr. J. J. Hill he controlled some 20,000 miles more. He was in entire harmony with the Pennsylvania (Standard Oil) group, controlling 14,000 miles; he had a community of interests with the Vanderbilts and Goulds and Mr. Harriman, thus having a grip on 110,000 out of the total of 190,000 miles of rail in the country.

The Standard Oil interests practically own the Pennsylvania Railroad, and Standard Oil investments predominate in the International Navigation Company, the aggressively American organization which owns the American and Red Star lines of steamers. Mr. Clement Griscom, the presiding genius of the International Company, was convinced that by adopting the principle of combination among Atlantic steamship services great savings could be effected. As a business man, it seemed to him ridiculous that three ships should leave New York in one day for Europe and then two or three days go by and none leave. He objected also to the cutting of rates that often went on.

The same idea occurred to Mr. B. N. Baker, President of the Atlantic Transport Line, a company representing very similar interests to the International Company. They persuaded financiers of the Standard Oil Company of the allied Widener electrical interests, and Mr. Pierpont Morgan to come in line with them. Both Mr. Morgan and the oil magnates felt that it was rather bad business for the American railroads to pay out over a hundred million dollars a year to foreign steamers for the continuance of the freight traffic which they gathered.

Then began a slow campaign. A syndicate was formed under Mr. Morgan, and about the same time a Shipping Subsidy Bill was actively pushed in the U.S. Congress. Alarmed by the Subsidy Bill, Mr. Ellerman, an exceedingly active British shipowner, and head of the Leyland Line, agreed to sell to Mr. Morgan the whole Leyland concern at what then seemed a very high figure, shares quoted in the market at £12 10s. being purchased for £14 10s. Mr. Morgan, it may be added, has since re-sold the line to his new company at a price showing a very large profit, so that he did not do quite so bad a bit of business as his critics thought.

The purchase of the Leyland Line was especially

fortunate. It removed from competition Mr. Ellerman, and it stopped the active freight war the Leyland Line had been waging on the Atlantic Transport. It further placed the syndicate in possession of an important line of steamers. Steps were immediately taken to develop the trade of the Leyland. Since the syndicate partly controlled the great American railways it was easy to open up a new grain trade at Quebec for Leyland boats, at the expense of the Eastern States of America.

By the spring of last year the syndicate had control of the American, Red Star, Atlantic Transport, and Leyland Lines. But the real struggle was yet to begin. Until the White Star and the two German Lines—the Hamburg-American and North German Lloyd—were brought in or neutralized, supremacy was impossible. The Cunard Line was less to be feared, for its business is more passenger than freight.

The main efforts of the syndicate were now directed at the White Star Line, but to conquer it was a formidable task. Its profits had been estimated not long before at a million pounds for one year. It was a private company, with a nominal capital of £750,000, and by its articles of association any shareholder wishing to sell had to offer his shares to the others. Above all, it was the pride and glory of the Ismay family, first among English shipowners. Mr. T. H. Ismay, but recently dead, had built up the line in his own lifetime, and his trustees held one-fifth of the shares. Members of the Ismay family held more.

When talk first arose of negotiations proceeding for the sale of the White Star Line, British shipping men were incredulous. Their unbelief was supported by repeated and emphatic denials by Mr. Bruce Ismay, the Managing Director of the line.

The syndicate were not at the end of their resources. Freight rates fell, so that the carriage of goods across the Atlantic ceased to be profitable. Mr. Pirrie, head of Harland and Wolff, the Belfast shipbuilders, builder of the White Star boats and largely interested in the White Star Line, was approached, and the danger of a railway war hung over the White Star directors.

It is easy enough, at this stage, to blame Mr. Bruce Ismay and his colleagues for joining the Americans, but the situation before them was anything but an enviable one. They knew that the American railroads could, if they desired, divert a large part of their traffic from them. Without the railroads the steamship lines would be robbed of four-fifths of their trade, and the railway lines were largely controlled by Mr. Morgan. The triumphs of previous years were no promise of future prosperity. Let the railways declare war and the White Star directors might struggle in vain. They must sell out or be beaten out of the field—and the Morgan syndicate were no hard buyers. They offered terms which might have proved attractive under any circumstances, and to some of the leaders of English shipping they offered greater power in the larger combine.

At the beginning of 1902 Mr. Ismay, Mr. Pirrie, the heads of the German lines, and other English shipping leaders went to New York. The gathering attracted great attention, and the public announcements that the meeting was only to come to an agreement on the freight question satisfied few. In February an arrangement was arrived at which made the Morgan syndicate supreme on the Atlantic, and which transferred the control of that ocean from England to America. The deal was kept quiet till late in April, when a guarded communication was made through the *Times* about it. At first it was hoped that the British company had only joined a mutual league. Assurances were given and greedily swallowed that the ships were still to be White Star boats and still to be under the British flag. This required no assurance, for it would have been folly for the syndicate to alter the flag, even had America permitted it. It is much cheaper to run boats under the British flag, and the White Star Line receives substantial subsidies from the British Government. Had the syndicate confessed the truth they might have admitted their fear lest the purchases of the line by a foreign company should make the British Government alter its relations to it.

When the terms of the agreement were issued in May it was seen that British prestige on the seas had received the most severe blow since before the days of Nelson. It was no combination that had been effected, but an absolute purchase, lock, stock, and barrel, by the Americans. And the agreement included more than this. It transferred the Dominion Line to Messrs. Morgan, and gave the company formed by them the entire right over the output

of the yard of Messrs. Harland and Wolff, the leading British shipbuilders.

Under the agreement between Messrs. J. P. Morgan and Co. and the heads of the steamship lines,
the White Star Line was bought, and all the business
of Ismay, Imrie and Co., except the Asiatic Steam
Navigation Company, for ten times the profits of
1900. The Dominion Line got the same terms. The
International Navigation Company was bought for
£6,831,600, while a large number of shares giving a
governing interest in the Leyland Line went at a
substantial advance upon the price paid in the sale
of 1901. The former owners of the White Star and
Dominion Lines bound themselves not to engage
in competitive trade for fourteen years.

It had already been announced that a working
arrangement was arrived at with the Hamburg-
American and North German Lloyd lines. An attempt was made last summer to secure control of
these lines also. A large amount of American capital
was employed in purchasing their shares. Seriously
alarmed, the German shipping chiefs held counsel
together. In England our shipowners were left to
themselves, the Government waiting to act until
the sale had been effected. In Germany the heads
of the two lines, Herr Ballin and Herr Plathe, met
the Kaiser last October, and after long conference a
plan was made by which the direction of the companies was confined to Germans living in Germany.
The German people were not going to allow themselves to be deprived of one of their national glories
by the power of an American syndicate. The pre-

caution was effectual. But even the Germans had
to consent to a working agreement. Had they not
done so the Americans would promptly have fought
them for their Mediterranean trade.

The sale of the White Star Line has stirred up
the English people as few industrial matters have
ever done. The nation realizes to some degree that
new powers have arisen, at whose bidding the course
of trade is changed. But we are setting about
meeting the new situation in a way scarcely worthy
of our national sense. There is a talk of a fresh
combine by which a number of old boats are to be
joined together as the British group in opposition
to the Morgans. It would be as satisfactory to
bombard Portsmouth forts with popguns.

CHAPTER IV

THE COMING SUBSIDIES

" The condition of the merchant marine calls for immediate remedial action. We should no longer have to submit to conditions under which only a trifling portion of our great commerce is carried on our own ships. From every standpoint it is unwise for the United States to continue to rely upon the ships of competing nations to distribute our goods."—PRESIDENT ROOSEVELT.

AMERICA has in the past failed to obtain a great ocean navy by ordinary means. It has for some time been cheaper to build vessels in England and to run them under the British flag than to build in America or to maintain under the Stars and Stripes. Given fair play and open competition there is little doubt but that the British could continue to lead. The latest American statistics show that during the last year more than one-half the imports to the United States brought there on steamships came under the British flag, and two-thirds of the exports were taken out by British ships. Of 1,255,000,000 tons of exports 846,000,000 were carried out on British vessels, as against 65,000,000 on American. Of 794,000,000 tons of imports 82,000,000 came in American steamships, as against 428,000,000 tons in British ships.

The greater cheapness of British ships is beyond question. Mr. B. N. Baker, head of the Atlantic Transport Line, placed contracts for ships with Harland and Wolff, of Belfast, the New York Shipbuilding Company, and the Maryland Steel Company. The largest of these boats were of a similar type to the big Atlantic liners, the *Minneapolis* and the *Minnehaha*—about 13,000 tons. The British cost £292,000 each : the New York Shipbuilding Company's price was £380,000. For smaller boats the Belfast firm charged £110,000 as against £150,000 by the Maryland Steel Company and the New York Shipbuilding Company.

The higher cost of running American ships was proved by some facts gathered by the United States Government about wages paid on vessels of a corresponding type. Comparing the American steamship *St. Louis* with the British *Oceanic* and the German *Kaiser Wilhelm der Grosse*, it was found that the *St. Louis*, having 380 men on its pay roll, cost in wages £2,260 ; the *Oceanic*, with 472 men on its pay roll, cost £1,980 ; and the *Kaiser Wilhelm der Grosse*, with 500 men, cost £1,543.

The same was shown in the report drawn up by Messrs. Holmer and Goodnough, recognized authorities on the question, about a plan to institute a large coal steamer service to Europe. It was proposed to build vessels of 6,500 gross and 4,400 nett tonnage, provided with all the latest facilities for carrying coal. The specialists reported that American vessels would be hopelessly out of competition. They gave two reasons—first the high cost, and next the " ridiculous employment laws." They showed by detailed figures that a vessel of the type proposed, when run under the American flag, would cost in wages £4,180 per year, as against £2,634 for an English vessel. The total operating cost under the American flag would be £32,699 per year, and under the English £26,605. The cost per ton of coal carried would be 7s. 6d. if a ship were American, as against 6s. 3d. if it were English. These experts reported in this instance that " there never was, nor is there now, any obstacle to the ownership of British vessels by Americans," and they recommended that the vessels should be run, if necessary, as British boats. This has already been done in many instances, and large numbers of really American ships—American, that is to say, so far as their ownership and management are concerned—are kept under the British flag. American citizens and companies to-day own over a million tons of foreign shipping, nearly all British.

The obvious means of counteracting the natural advantages British traders possess is to allow American owners a subsidy. This session Senator Frye, of Maine, brought before Congress a Bill providing for this. His Bill passed the Senate, but was dropped in the Lower House owing to fear of public opinion in the West and fear of the results such a law would have on the coming autumn elections. Yet though Senator Frye's Bill has disappeared the subject is

bound to revive, and it is well we should face it.
Senator Frye proposed that ships receiving subsidies
must be American built, employing American
officers, and with so far as possible American crews.
He proposed to give, apart from special mail subsidies, a bounty of a halfpenny per gross ton per
hundred nautical miles sailed. This bounty he calculated would completely counterbalance the present
British advantage. It is difficult to overestimate
the importance of such a proposal, and the far-
reaching results it must have when it passes into
law. In this country we are slowly awakening to
its importance, but even many shippers at present
are careless about it. " You are stirring too soon,"
said one merchant to me. " You must wait till our
shipping is lost to us. Then we will begin to debate
the matter, and our Government will appoint a
Royal Commission to investigate, but not until
then."

I have made opportunity of obtaining the views
of many prominent English shipowners on the effects
of a proposal such as this. Naturally the shipowners do not care, for obvious business reasons, that
their names should be quoted. Yet their views are
well worth studying without their names. The first
who writes to me is the managing director of a well-
known Transatlantic passenger and freight line.
Says he : " If a United States Subsidy Bill only
grants subsidies to steamers built by United States
shipbuilders, and manned by United States crews,
I do not think it will *at first* materially affect British
interests, except by increasing the already heavy

competition in the North Atlantic trade. With experience no doubt the United States shipbuilders will be able to produce as cheaply as the shipbuilders in the United Kingdom, and United States shipping companies will be able to effect economies in wages and other directions. Then of course the unsubsidized British steamer would have to give up the United States trade ; and not merely the United States but Canada also will be affected, because cargo and passengers can even now be freighted as cheaply *viâ* the United States ports of Boston, Portland, and New York as by the Canadian ports.

" If the Subsidy Bill is to enable the Morgan alliance to obtain subsidies on British-built steamers in consideration of their adding a certain percentage of American-built tonnage, these disastrous results would begin at once ; and without some counterveiling subsidies from the British Government the North American trade from the Gulf of St. Lawrence to the Gulf of Mexico would be lost to British shipping."

Here is a pessimistic opinion from a London house : " There is a tendency in some quarters to underestimate the effects that an American Shipping Subsidies Bill will have if it passes into law. We think this regrettable, because we say confidently that we have never known any measure passed by any nation more calculated to do injury to British interests. Some of those most qualified to speak on the matter have openly expressed their opinion that the whole of the British freight trade is seriously menaced. In our opinion if the Bill (Senator Frye's) passes through into law as it stands at present it will be the end of this trade. The one thing for us to do would be for us to sell our ships to the successful Yankees as soon as possible. The action of those who sold out to Mr. Pierpont Morgan and others some time ago was considerably criticized. They certainly knew what they were about, and they made an excellent bargain. It was a case of audacious foresight thoroughly justified. One cannot help wondering whether the American purchasers were as satisfied with the transaction as were the English managers.

" One fears that it is too late to talk vaguely of remedies. If we had a Government with the slightest perception of the supreme importance of commercial matters, or if we had men in power who had any real knowledge of business, there might still be hope of some thorough and immediate action to meet the threatening state of affairs. No man, however, who thinks of the constitution of a Government such as the present, would look in this direction for any help whatever. A bounty to English ships, subsidizing them as much as their rivals would be subsidized, is the only rational answer to America's new move. They know what they are about. Why cannot our people have at least sufficient knowledge to be able to answer so unmistakable a challenge ? If one could see a bounty on corn added to this bounty on ships one would be still better pleased.

" We estimate the effects will be most felt in three directions. (1) The mileage subsidy will encourage the Americans first of all to attack all branches of the long-distance trade. As experienced shippers we expect that their first attempt will be to control the trade of the far East. (2) We believe subsidies will encourage the growth of a vast mercantile marine. This will to some very considerable extent do away with the advantage which we undoubtedly possess on this side of being able to turn out ships faster, better, and cheaper than our rivals can do. Not only can we beat the Americans here, but we can beat every other nation. Shipbuilding is specially dear in France, and the work is far from satisfactory when done as far as the individual workman is concerned. Yet the subsidies given by the Government have lent a tremendous impetus to the building of ships in that country. It may be mentioned that of the sailing ships leaving England, especially for long-distance voyages, quite an extraordinary proportion are French. This applies particularly to Cardiff and Liverpool. (3) The subsidies for speed will tend to make these merchant vessels veritable clippers. We have had experience already of the way in which they can affect our trade, for until the Civil War American ships were very dangerous competitors with ours.

" At the same time it is almost ironical to see exactly what is going to be done without being able to help ourselves. Every practical man can see that this Shipping Subsidy Bill is only meant to be temporary. It is a case of helping the child to walk until it is able to run by itself, and while this process is going on it is hoped that such blows will be dealt to the shipping of other countries that when the inevitable withdrawal of the grant occurs American shipping will be in such a position, and have such a hold over the carrying trade of the world, that outside competition will not be of much avail.

" It should be noted that the subsidies will affect different lines in different ways. Passenger steamers will at first scarcely be affected at all. It is the freight trade that is aimed at. Indirectly also it can be seen that it is part of a great national commercial policy, and we must look as much to the department of manufacture and general industry for the final effects of the Subsidy Bill, as to the more direct sphere of shipping."

It will be well perhaps to quote with one less pessimistic forecast. I give this from another London shipowner :

" One department of British shipping which an American Subsidy Bill will be powerless to affect, whatever it may do in other directions, is our coasting trade. Whether it will affect any departments seriously is none too certain if we reason by analogy, and remembering the scare that the passing of the French and the German Subsidy Bills gave us. Then it was said over and over again that the two subsidized nations would sweep the seas. What, however, has been the actual result ? Germany has her ships for sale at any price, and France has found that the promise of the bounties has not fulfilled expectations confidently raised. It is worth noting that only two French lines have really benefited to any appreciable extent by these aids. These are the Messageries Maritimes and the American liners. The success of the latter has not been totally inimical to us. We built some of their best ships at Greenock, and built others for them at St. Nazaire, part of the agreement made being that we should lay down a yard there so as to show them how ships were to be built. In one department the French grants have had a notable effect in calling into existence a splendid fleet of large sailing ships.

"But our coasting trade is impregnable. It is defended in several ways. The freights are ridiculously low. We have to go down to bed-rock prices owing to the competition of the Yorkshire and the Durham districts in selling their gas coal. We recoup ourselves by the cargoes of colonial and other goods which we carry back on the return journey. We have the advantage of getting into the ports at lower rates than other steamers. A coasting steamer is very much less heavily charged than one from a foreign port. Take Liverpool as an example. Two instances of different goods will show the effect. Raw wool pays 1s. 2d. a ton when brought in by a coasting steamer, and 3s. when from a foreign port. Copper also is similarly cheaper. The coaster pays 1s. a ton, and the others 2s. 4d. Even if a steamer has put into an English port before proceeding to Liverpool, or whatever port she may have cargo for, she is still considered as coming from a foreign port. We have to meet the competition of several large lines already, and it is partly to this fact that we are able to compete successfully. The addition of any number of American lines to this competition would make no difference.

"Would the bounty given then, we ask, be sufficient

to overcome the difference in the charges ? Even
if it did we have still another rampart to defend us.
This is the question of time. Before the big ship
can be unloaded and started again, we have had
our goods and delivered them. It pays no one to
wait when they can have their consignments without
delay. Again, supposing an American vessel wanted
to get on even terms in the matter of port dues—
there is a way. She would have to unload every
item of cargo and re-ship them for the other port.
This would at once add to the delay and to the
expense in another direction. There would be quay
dues to pay.

" However, even supposing that all these ram-
parts were carried, a final one remains, and this is
practically insurmountable. The Americans do not
know the trade. They might have ship following
ship from port to port; they might cut prices as
much as they liked ; they might cover the ground
as thoroughly as they liked ; but unless they sat
where we sit, in our own offices, they could not get
the trade. It is the knowledge that this man will
want so many bags of sugar carried at such and such
a date to such and such a place, that another will
have copper for carriage, another want a consign-
ment of wool, that brings trade. This knowledge
subsidies cannot convey, and no number of bought
ships can give to their purchasers. In other words,
it is the business that matters and not the instruments by means of which that business is carried
out. This is where the American cuteness was apparent in the Leyland Line deal. They bought the

business, the goodwill, the connexion. Had the ships merely been bought, Mr. Ellerman might have sold them by the hundred, and still kept all the essential parts in his own hands. I should be willing to sell as many ships as were wanted by any one who chose to buy them. I could replace them all at a week's notice and have them in running order within ten days. So, taking it all round, I think we may say that our coasting trade need fear no invaders. If the Americans want to buy up our businesses, that is another matter. Has any one ever met a business man who was averse to concluding a transaction provided he stood to benefit by it in a manner which he considered adequate ? Probably all of us would sell on terms.

" If we take the broader field of shipping in general, there is one thing worthy of notice. The cost of building ships on the other side of the Atlantic is already considerably higher than it is here. This disparity will increase. In business language this means that American shipowners will have to capitalize their subsidies in order to pay for the extra expenditure in building their ships. This being so, the competition is fair and level. Honours are easy.

" The one great advantage the American ships possess is having so many harbours on the coast which are capable of receiving vessels of 10,000 tons. This means large ports, large ships, large cargoes. A cargo of 10,000 tons can be more economically handled than one of 1,000 tons. This explains to some extent the remarkably cheap freights which have been quoted for the Atlantic carriage of coals to French and Mediterranean ports."

The following is the exact text of Mr. B. N. Baker's letter to the United States Commissioner of Navigation :—

ATLANTIC TRANSPORT LINE, OFFICE OF THE PRESIDENT.
BALTIMORE,
October 17, 1901.

DEAR MR. CHAMBERLAIN,—Referring to my letter of March 16, 1901, and replying to your request with regard to relative difference in cost of ships, our company at present have a contract for two ships with Harland and Wolff, Limited, Belfast (one of which will be completed very early in the spring and the other a little later, say during the summer), of exactly the same size, dimensions, and all particulars as two ships we have contracted for with the New York Shipbuilding Company, of Camden. The cost of the English-built ship, as near as possible (we having just completed two of exactly the same size, dimensions, and speed), will be about £292,000 ($1,419,120). The same identical ship built at the works of the New York Shipbuilding Company will cost us a little over £380,000 ($1,846,800).

In addition to this we are building two steamers with the New York Shipbuilding Company of smaller dimensions, for which we have a contract at £150,000 each ($729,000) ; also two ships of exactly the same dimensions with the Maryland Steel Company, Sparrow's Point, for £150,000 each ($729,000). We have two ships of identically the same detail, delivered to us in the last twelve months, built by Harland and Wolff, Belfast, one of which cost me £110,000 ($534,000), and the other £100,000 ($486,000).

Very truly yours,
B. N. BAKER, President.

EUGENE T. CHAMBERLAIN, ESQ., Commissioner of Navigation, Washington, D. C.

Senator Frye's own summary of his Subsidies Bill,

read to the Senate Committee on Commerce, ran thus :—

"The establishment of this complete American ocean mail service, involving much shipbuilding, will require several years. It will render the United States as independent of foreign Powers for its ocean mail service as is Great Britain. The cost of the American service by American mail steamers will be $4,700,000. The cost of the British and Colonial service by British mail steamers is $4,700,000; Receipts from ocean postage by the United States are now estimated at $3,000,000. The annual deficit under the new American system proposed, including minor services, will be about $2,000,000. The annual deficit under the British Colonial system is $2,188,000. The postal subsidy provisions enable the Postmaster-General to establish an American ocean mail system superior to the systems of Great Britain, France, and Germany. The American ocean mail system outlined contemplates on the Pacific weekly mail service to Hawaii, the Philippines, Japan, China, and Hong Kong, and a fortnightly service to Pago Pago, New Zealand, and Australia. The maximum cost would be $2,335,000. On the Atlantic the Bill contemplates semi-weekly mail services to Jamaica, Havana, and Europe ; weekly to Mexico ; once in ten days to Venezuela ; and fortnightly to Brazil, at a maximum cost of $2,365,000. The report compares in detail American services proposed with British services, and asserts that the Bill will revolutionize in American favour as against the Suez route the world's ocean mail connexions with China and Japan, and will affect Australian connexions. It will give the United States forty-two auxiliary merchant cruisers compared with Great Britain's fifty.

"The second part of the report deals with the general subsidy to all American vessels, steam and sail, except mail steamers. It quotes President Roosevelt's message, showing that the cost of building American ships is greater than the cost of building ships abroad ; that American wages on shipboard are higher, and that the Government should remedy these inequalities. Discriminating duties, export bounties, and subsidies based on export cargoes are in violation of our international obligations, so direct subsidies is the only practical method. The subsidy proposed is not a naked bounty, for it is based on public services to be rendered in return. Americans have absolute free trade in foreign-going ships, so no shipbuilders' trust is possible under the Bill. Shipbuilders can import now free of duty materials for ships for foreign trade, so no combination to raise prices of materials is practicable. If an American shipowner will build his vessel in the United States, employing home labour, employing American officers and crew, performing certain services for the American Government, and using the vessel to promote American commerce, he will be paid a subsidy sufficient to put him on an equality with the foreign shipowner, employing foreign labour and serving a foreign Government. The average cost of building ocean steamers, mainly for cargo, is $102 per ton in the United States, and $76 in Great Britain. Average monthly wages on monthly steamers, mainly for cargo, are : American $36, British $26, German and Scandinavian $17. The general subsidies proposed equalize American and foreign costs on these bases.

" The Bill will promote the building of new vessels of large carrying capacity, which promote export trade at low freight rates. Combined with our geographical position, it gives special advantages to American vessels in the Pacific trade. Based on actual navigation of American vessels in foreign trade in 1900, the subsidies proposed would amount to $1,072,000, divided as follows : Steam (excluding mail vessels), $559,000 ; sail, $513,000. Geographically—Atlantic Ocean, $440,000 ; Pacific, $427,000 ; square-rigged ships on both oceans, $161,000. Full compliance with all requirements for the Bill would fix the initial expenditures at between $800,000 and $900,000. Under the general subsidy increase in expenditures depends on increase in shipbuilding. The completion of 200,000 tons of ocean steamers for foreign trade in one year, involving $1,300,000 in subsidies, will place the United States in advance of Germany as a shipbuilding nation.''

CHAPTER V

FOUR years ago American boots were practically unknown in this country. To-day they form the most prominent display in our shoe shops from Dover to Aberdeen. Sales have gone up fivefold in four years, and the total value of imports of this article was £369,437 in 1901. The Americans have also taken an appreciable part of our export shoe trade from us. In Australia, which was once largely supplied from England, British imports have declined, while the demand for American shoes has doubled in four years. In France the trade has increased nearly threefold in two years, and the total export trade from America to there rose 63 per cent. between 1899 and 1901.

The failure of our shoe manufacturers to meet successfully American competition has filled Northampton and Leeds and Leicester with workless men. It has meant want and poverty for many who not long since were earning respectable incomes. Up to quite recently our shoe manufacturers stubbornly refused to admit that the Americans were at all serious rivals, and even now they give them the most grudging recognition. For the past year their trade organs have been full of articles denouncing American competition as a bogey, and as mere blustering pretence. To scoff at it has been the favourite occupation at their banquets. They evidently think that if they deny its existence long enough and loudly enough it will disappear. Yet this fight has only begun. The leading Transatlantic shoe manufacturers are now here in person to push their trade. Several of them have opened their own shops, which they run on very attractive lines, with clever advertising devices to attract attention. Some of the more far-sighted of the English traders are adopting the American name and the American style. One large house, well known in Northampton, runs a number of its retail branches under the title of an American shoe company. Not long since it took action against an American who was manufacturing " American " shoes in Leicester to prevent him calling himself American in such a way as to appear to resemble them.

The chief American business, however, is done through ordinary retailers. A leading English journal, *The Shoe and Leather Record*, issues a supplement solely devoted to the wares and methods of our rivals. The British trade, while laughing at the Americans, is cutting its prices and altering its methods to meet them, but British sales are going down and American are ever on the increase.

The sale of manufactured shoes, important as it

is in one way, is really the least part of the American conquest of our leather trade. A few years since three men met in a room in New York City, and resolved to wage a war of conquest on the world in general. The free-booting barons of old planted their castles on the tops of hills, at the end of valleys, and exacted toll by force of arms from all passing travellers. The castle of these modern barons was an office in a great New York building. In place of arms they had brains, honesty and ingenuity. But though their methods were different the results are the same. To-day they and their representatives are exacting toll out of almost every person in England and America, and out of a very large proportion of the dwellers on the Continent of Europe.

Who are they? Their names are certainly not known to fame outside of their own particular trade; yet the way they have won the world is one of the romances of commerce. They are the " United Shoe Machinery Company."

Their plan of campaign was this. In America they amalgamated many leading firms, and acquired most of the great master patents in shoe manufacturing machinery. Shoemaking has long emerged from the stage of being a simple process, and few articles of every-day use require so many mechanical processes. It is said that the better class shoe goes through nearly one hundred machines from first to last before it is completed, each of them different, and most of them of very elaborate character.

After combining the leading firms in America the boot barons came over to Europe and established

their special representative, Mr. Connor, in Frank-
fort, from where he practically controls the affairs
of this continent for them.   In England they bought
up firm after firm in this line of business.   It is said
that they prefer to pay cash where possible, but if
necessary they allow desired firms into the combination on shares.   Such great houses as Pierson
and Benyon, the English and American Machinery
Company, the Union Machine Company, and Goodyear and Company were amalgamated, and the British
United Machinery Company was established.   In
France they formed the " United Machinery Company de France," and in Germany another company
was formed.   Keen business men in this country
saw that it was better to work with the great trust
than against it, and so many of them threw their
forces on its side.

Then the company set itself deliberately to compel
British manufacturers to use its supplies.   It had a
hard task, and had it not been backed up by the
undoubted excellence of its machines it must have
failed.   The regulations of the trade union did not
encourage quicker machinery, and many manufacturers were welded to old methods.   But even
the most conservative maker sees in time that he
cannot afford to use a machine which makes, say,
500 button-holes in an hour, and requires three processes to do it, when he can get another that will
make 3,000 an hour with only one process.

It was such superiority as this that drove our
manufacturers, willing or unwilling, to buy.   The
United Company does not as a rule sell outright.

It leases its machines for a low payment down and a royalty on production. For instance, one of its machines for wire stitching can be had free of cost on condition that the wire used is bought from the combination. The company in this way now secures various royalties on almost every pair of shoes made in England. The mediaeval barons were mere bunglers compared with the enlightened business men of to-day.

Such enterprise has of course encountered serious opposition, but the very success of the United Company enables it to hold the field. There are various British inventors trying to outdo it, but it controls master patents which hamper any imitators. And the British inventor knows as a rule that he can secure better terms from the combination than he can by fighting it. What is more, it is so busy devising improvements that by the time one machine has become public property, owing to the expiration of its patent, it is out of date, and a new apparatus has been placed on the market which outdoes it. By the excellence of their machines these American over-lords have secured supremacy in our trade.

The introduction of American labour-saving machinery is doubtless an economic gain to us. But the most optimistic can scarcely believe that the importation in large quantities of American shoes, as apart from American shoe machinery, is anything but a loss to British trade. Not many months since it was the fashion to denounce American competition in the shoe trade as a " lath painted to look like iron." We were told that it was a mere passing fad, that would go in a few months. In the late autumn of last year, when I was at Northampton, masters and workmen alike had one story. " We are tired of hearing of these American shoes," they said. " The whole thing is an American dodge, and what success the Americans have had is solely through bragging. Wait till the winter comes. Do you think the thin American shoes will ever stand our climate ? Not a bit of it. American shoes will fill English churchyards. It is mere nonsense to regard them as dangerous to us."

Yet as the men were telling me this the state of affairs in their own town might well have bidden them pause For a thousand houses were empty. Over two thousand people were on the books of the Guardians in the Poor Law district for out-door relief at that time. Large numbers of factories were working—as they have been right through the winter—short time, and men ordinarily earning 28s. a week were, I found in many cases, earning 9s. or 12s., while girls usually paid 12s. or 14s. a week were only making 5s. or 6s. The children of the poor went hungry to school, and a town relief fund had been started for the unemployed. Twice within the past few weeks crowds had assembled outside the workhouse gates demanding work. On the first day of my visit to the town a man had been taken before the magistrate for breaking a shop window. " Send me to prison," he said ; " I can get no work ; I am starving. Anything is better than this." And that same week at a Town's Meeting, presided over by the Mayor, and called to consider the question of the unemployed, one speaker had declared that, " The authorities must either find work for the unemployed workmen, or must take upon themselves the more serious responsibility still of introducing to the town a regiment of soldiers to keep the men in order. There are times when patience is a crime, and this is one of them. (Applause and dissent.) If my friends and fellow workers are content to stand quietly by and see men and women and children starve, I am not. (Applause.) Work or food is our cry, and we mean to have it."

That very year a great American last factory had sprung up in the town itself, and one of the largest of the local buyers and manufacturers was stocking his shops with American wares. The manufacturers themselves were adopting American patterns on a wholesale scale, throwing aside the old British style, and shoes were being made in Leicester, if not in Northampton, in imitation of American wares, to be sold as American goods. The whole matter was summarized from the official reports of the Northamptonshire Union of Boot and Shoe Operatives for November, 1901. The general report of this Union says : " Since sending out our last report the returns we have received from a large majority of our branches do not give anything like a favourable account of the condition of the trade. Generally speaking, the secretaries report that it is very bad and quiet. In fact some of the branches have found it necessary not only to pay the contributions of some of their members who have been out of employment for weeks, and in some instances months, but have granted large sums from their funds to assist members out of work. From the general appearance of trade all round we are not likely to be in for a boom yet awhile." The Local Union at Northampton wrote : " Trade is still very bad in the town, the number of unemployed having increased since the October report, in addition to which many of those in work are only earning about sufficient to pay rent."

There was great hope in the trade that springtime would see an improvement. There is usually a rush of spring orders, but in the spring of 1902 this rush did not come. In March the condition of things was really serious. Short time was general not only in Northampton, but in Leeds and Leicester and other centres. In Northampton the Mayor was stopped by a crowd of the unemployed one Sunday when returning from an official visit to church, and threatened with violence by the men, who said they were starving. Four of the ringleaders were prosecuted. In court they refused to apologize, saying that there were hundreds of men going without bread in their town, and that they were working for them. In Leeds some factories abandoned the farce of opening their doors. The financial strain was severely felt, and even the various shoe-trade journals, which usually paint things in the most roseate hues, now print week after week details of undeniable distress. " Is this the beginning of the end ? " one trade paper asked, after telling something of the prevalent slackness.

The American imports continued to grow, as they do at the time of writing this. Right through the winter months, despite the cry that American shoes would fill British churchyards, they came more and more into use. During the month of January American boots and shoes to the value of £32,000 were sent to the United Kingdom, as against £23,000 in January, 1901. In April they came to £53,600, as against £45,000 in 1901. For the ten months ending April their value was £335,900, as against £229,000 in the corresponding period ending April, 1901, and £143,100 in 1900. In January and February British exports of British boots and shoes declined from 121,011 dozen in the same time in 1901, to 116,022 dozen. Nothing but the abnormal demand in South Africa prevented the decline being more marked, for there were decreases shown under every heading in the British official returns except South Africa and " other countries."

How is it that the Americans have been able to take from us an appreciable section of our home trade, and still more of our foreign, at a time when our well-stocked factories are partly closed ? Much is undoubtedly due to the fact that American boots are finer and more stylish than English wares at corresponding prices. They fit better, and Americans study their customers in a way which English makers up to quite recently did not do. For instance, they provide half sizes and will give half a dozen widths as a matter of course.

The makers across the Atlantic obtain a much greater output with the same machinery and number of hands, and American manufacturers claim that they can turn out three pairs of boots for two finished by Englishmen. Even in Northampton it is admitted that the American output with the corresponding machinery is much higher than ours. Apparently both masters and men are responsible for this. The American manufacturer specializes. The English manufacturer attempts to make all kinds of footwear. In an American factory men can be kept on one machine, and perhaps at one or two sizes of last, and consequently they obtain far greater dexterity than when they have, as in England, to manage several different sizes. The American manufacturer also prepares his work more thoroughly for the men than is done in England.

English makers declare that the Union deliberately limits output, and refuses to allow the machines to be worked to their full capacity. While there is little or no evidence that this is done by the Union as such, it must be granted that the English workers in the shoe trade do not exert themselves as Americans do. This point is practically yielded in a recent report of the Northampton branch of the National Union of Boot and Shoe Operatives, where it is said : " It is to be regretted that the Employers' Federation still harp upon restriction of output by the workers, while they themselves are the main and principal cause of restriction, if such a thing does exist. We ask the members of such a body how in any common fairness they can expect men with only the minimum wage to live upon, and the expenses of town life, to turn out the same amount of work as an American does, when they themselves tell us that American wages are so much higher than our own rate of pay ?   If a man has a low rate of wages he must be compelled to live upon poorer food than a man with high wages.   Let the manufacturers, therefore, instead of filling up their report with this padding year by year, do what lies in their power to do—that is, pay higher wages so that a man can get the best of food, and thereby increase his mental and physical powers to enable him to increase output, if that is the desideratum aimed at."

A somewhat similar defence of the working man was made to me by Mr. E. L. Poulton, President of the Northampton Council, and local leader of the Trades Unionists.   Mr. Poulton, with evident sincerity, emphatically denied that to-day, whatever might have been true in the past, the Union encourages the men to " ca' canny."

" Those who charge the Northampton workman with being an idler and the Union with limiting output are wrong," he said.   " Go in our factories here, and you will see work being carried on at a rate that would surprise many of our competitors.   It is said that the output of American workmen in the shoe trade is greater than that of the English with the same machinery.   If this is true, there are many reasons to account for it.

" First comes the climate.   The American atmosphere is drier and more stimulating, making greater exertion possible.   Then, the American workman is paid more.   According to the statements of the masters he earns twice as much.   Now a better-paid man is a better-fed man, and when a worker has a higher standard of living he is capable of doing more work.

" If English masters would pay American wages, and would prepare the bottom stuff in the same way the Americans do, they would get American output.   The houses here that pay the highest wages make no complaint of the output of their men.   But it is the firms that pay 28s. or 30s. a week, the usual wage here, which expect to get the work of a £3 man. They cannot do it.   A man paid the minimum wage has no incentive to special industry.

" One often hears," continued Mr. Poulton, " of cases of men who have been on piece, and who by straining themselves to the utmost have made as much as 45s. a week.   The employers have put them at day work at 30s. a week, expecting the same output.   They do not get it, not because the Trade Union makes any restriction, but because conditions under piece and day work are entirely different.

" The different arrangement of the factories in the two countries also partly accounts for the smaller output here per man.   In America one man attends to one class of machine, and often one size and style of last.   The American factory as a rule specializes in a few styles of boots.   Here firms attempt to make a multitude of kinds.   Now a man who has to attend to four or five varieties of machines, and who has to work on varied lasts, cannot do so much as the one who is always working at one thing.   The specialist is bound to be faster.

" As to whether the arrangements of the factories

could not be improved, that is not the business of
the workman.   You must go to the manufacturers
about that.   They insist on the right to conduct
their own business in their own way.   This right was
respected and accepted in 1895.   What we ask is
good wages for our work, and as to how the work
shall be planned and managed—we leave that to the
employer.

" Not long since one of the big manufacturers here
told me," Mr. Poulton asserted, " that if one of his
men were to attempt to dispute with him he would
turn him out of the factory at once, even though
the man were right and he wrong.   ' I will not be
answered back in my own factory,' he said.   Now,
when employers assume this position, how can you
expect the men to think out improvements ? "

At the very time when distress was most acute
one section of Northamptonshire workmen showed
an example of stupid conservatism which it would
be hard to beat.   Messrs. Nichols, of Raunds, introduced a new American lasting machine into their
factory, and the riveters and finishers rose in a body
one morning to exclude three men who were coming
to work the new machines.   The strangers were
persuaded to return home, and the old hands
marched through the town with flags flying and
band at their head.   They went outside the works
of makers thought favourable to the improved
machines, hooting and booing and groaning, and
in one case throwing dirt and stones.

The employers explained that they had practically
no option in the matter.   They were compelled by

contracts to get this work done quickly. As they could not induce their men to work sufficiently to meet their demands they had to have faster machinery. The operatives, who can earn in three days sufficient to keep them for a week, had showed no readiness to help the contractors to do their work in the time required. This case affords an illustration of what I said earlier, that the Trade Union was not responsible for the reactionary policy of the men, for they were non-Unionists. They had refused to join the Union because it was too strict for them, and the Union would certainly have opposed such action as they took.

A writer in the *Northampton Daily Reporter*, said by the editor to be a prominent local shoe manufacturer, summarized the case against the British methods last August. After referring to those who were content with existing things as living in a " fool's paradise," he went on to say : " American boots have been sent into this country in increasing quantities the last five years. Do they find favour with the general public ? I say most emphatically that they do. . . . The American boots have been most admired because of their particular quality. They have followed closely the best West End London style ; the fit has been perfect ; they have been exceptionally light of hand and comfortable to wear ; the materials have been of the lightest and finest —in some cases leather which no manufacturer has been able to obtain here.

" The present is an age of machinery not only in our own but in every other of wholesale manufacture.

That trade has benefited the most that has been able
to utilize machinery to its full capacity. How do we
stand in relation to this ? Nearly the whole of the
machinery we use is of American production ; in
fact to use only English would spell ruin. We stand
at a great disadvantage in this matter, for naturally
the country that has made and invented the machines will know how to use them to the best advantage. Northampton manufacturers have bought
largely American machines. Are they used to their
full capacity, and is the quality of work such as they
are capable of doing ? I say distinctly no. In no
case is work produced on them such as is sent over
to this country by American manufacturers in best
goods. There are not made by any firm in the town
best goods wholly by machinery such as is sent over
here.

" Northampton manufacturers have been using
every effort to adopt the American methods, but
up to the present with very little success. The two
systems of business are entirely different. The
American knows very well that if he is to reap the
full benefit of his machinery he must specialize,
and therefore he confines his business to one particular class of goods only, and very often at one
price. The Northampton manufacturer on the contrary makes men's, women's, and children's goods
in great variety and at all prices, and has therefore
very much more detail to attend to.

" Work in the American factory is minutely sub-
divided, and, in addition to this, certain parts used
in the production of boots are prepared by a separate

manufacturer entirely. Heels, stiffeners, toe puffs, welting, and many other things are made quite a distinct business, and are supplied to the boot manufacturer better than he could prepare them himself. This also relieves him of the trouble of supervising their preparation. The American is able to produce the best class of work in such a manner that I venture to say no English firm can produce regardless of cost. Owing to the sub-division of work the American workman gets very proficient in the particular part he is confined to, and is able to work at a much quicker pace.

"Are American boots cheaper than English, quality for quality, price for price? I say yes. They have no difficulty in beating us from one to two shillings per pair in medium and better class goods. The reason for this is explained by the cost of production. Owing to the facility for making their goods by the aid of machinery the cost of wages per pair is from $12\frac{1}{2}$ per cent. to 20 per cent. less than here. All their workmen are paid by piece work, and earn much higher wages than our own, while the cost per pair is much less than here. I think every manufacturer who has been there, and those who have a personal knowledge of their methods, will say their men are able to do a much larger quantity of work than is done here. It costs more to make a common men's machine-sewn glacé boot on the Northampton statement than it does a best men's welted in the States. Mr. John Hanan, a director of the Goodyear Company, and also an American manufacturer, some years ago published his wages statement for making and finishing best men's goods, which was at least 1s. 3d. less per pair than the Northampton statement, and he stated that goods of equal quality were made at much less cost than this price. This has never been disputed. The Trade Union has been in a great measure responsible for this. The officials have done all in their power to prevent the machinery being used to its full extent, and have helped to keep wages much lower than they would have been. What are the results ? Our export trade has almost disappeared, with the exception of South Africa, and is not nearly so large as it was twenty years ago. To remedy this state of things the suggestion I would make is to bring over here a number of experienced foremen who will train our workmen in better methods.. Fight the Union tooth and nail in their Socialistic programme of restricting the output, and by this means the wages of our men could be increased considerably, and we should be enabled to meet any foreign competition and largely increase our export trade."

The English shoe trade is slowly waking up. Now it is becoming quite in the order of things to find even among the manufacturers themselves a few leading men openly telling others of the stupidity and short-sightedness of the methods British firms employed in the past. The lines of reform necessary here are clear to any one who investigates the trade. Unless our manufacturers are willing to specialize, and unless masters and men adopt a policy of piece work or premiums for extra production, our trade must suffer.   Yet there is no reason whatever why, by adopting the improvements which foreign experience has shown to be advantageous, we should not win back all we have lost and that quickly. For, despite all, British manufacture has many advantages which, rightly used, should count for much. The British shoe operative, if he were a little more ambitious and were content to drink a little less, need fear no man.   The technical skill of the Northampton shoemaker is far-famed to-day, and technical skill goes a long way.

But there is one way in which we will make no gain.   A leading organ of the industry last winter inserted a signed letter by a London trader advocating tactics which, if allowed to go on, will destroy the chief asset of English commerce—honesty of production.   England has in the past, with rare exceptions, left false trade marks and scamped work to minor rivals.   Unfortunately the attitude taken in this letter, so far as I have seen, met with no repudiation from the trade.   In discussing American competition in footwear this shoe merchant says : " I am quite old enough in my trade experience to remember the French invasion of the late sixties and early seventies. . . . Though I am without reliable statistics, I am of opinion that the importation of French shoes reached figures which the American have not yet achieved. . . . Well, how did we deal with this trouble ? Simply by giving the public what they asked for—French (?) boots, stamped with French sizes, and—should one be ashamed to confess it ?—with French names and labels, conceived

in more or less bad French. In the end the 'invasion' was killed by ridicule, for the lowest pro-
ductions of Whitechapel and that ilk were introduced as 'modes de Paris,' and gradually the public
reverted to its old love."

CHAPTER VI

IRON AND STEEL

THERE are times when figures sum up a history in more effective fashion than any description. The statistics of iron and steel production in Great Britain and America afford an example of this. Ten years ago England was by far the largest producer of steel and iron in the world, and her supremacy seemed beyond competition. America took each year large quantities of our hard metals, and our manufactured steel goods went everywhere, and everywhere had the name of being the best.

Take pig iron, which Sir Christopher Furness recently,[1] paraphrasing Beaconsfield's famous saying, declared to be even more than the consumption of chemicals, an index of national progress, prosperity and civilization. In 1884 England produced nearly twice as much pig iron as the United States ; by 1900 America had caught us up. In 1899, our record year, we produced 9,305,500 tons, while America then surpassed us with 13,838,634 tons.

[1] *Pall Mall Magazine*, March, 1902.

Since then American production has rapidly risen, and ours both absolutely and relatively declined. Up to the early summer of last year America was selling its surplus in the very heart of our manufacturing districts. This is no longer so, owing to the unequalled home demand in America, and Americans are now actually buying largely in our markets. But the production of each nation for last year was—England (estimated), 8,200,000 tons ; the United States, 15,878,354. These figures require no comment. One State in America alone, Pennsylvania, produced within as much by a few hundred thousand tons as England. The Americans are now expecting to reach immediately a monthly capacity in their blast furnaces of 1,500,000 tons a month.

A very similar state of affairs is found in the production of steel. In five years the American output of steel has increased between two and threefold. In 1896 the total output was 5,218,606 : last year the figures had risen to 13,369,611 tons. Our output was less than five million tons.

It is to-day literally true that America holds the world's steel market at its mercy. For the moment American competition is not severely felt in other lands. The great home production, the activity in railway construction, building and shipping, give a home market for all the country can produce. But this condition of things is not going to last. Production, rapidly on the increase, is bound soon to exceed home consumption. Then America once more will compete for the outer markets, and will compete with such advantages as will enable her to carry all before her unless our methods are re-organized.

Last autumn I was crossing the ocean with the special representative of a distant Government, who had been examining the works of the great producers in England and America before giving certain big orders. We were talking on the methods of the two countries, and he declared with conviction : " I have come fresh from the plants of both lands, going straight from England to America. All I can say is this : the British plants and equipment are like toys compared with the American. It only needs any British iron master to examine for himself to see this."

My companion spoke truly. And, though he did not know it at the time, British ironmasters had already been over, and were preparing for the coming fight. The year 1901 was marked by the awakening of the British iron trade. The first great sign of this was the long visit of Mr. Arthur Keen, head of the firm of Guest, Keen and Co., to America, accompanied by his colleague, Mr. E. Windsor Richards. It is significant that Mr. Keen should have undertaken this, for he is a veteran of commerce, well over seventy years old. His Dowlais works have long been known as among the best equipped and most prosperous in this country.

While Mr. Keen was in America he was maturing a scheme for a combination of British iron masters, to meet the great American combination then being formed. His return home was quickly followed by fresh moves. New mining rights were acquired in

Spain, the Cyfarthfa iron works were absorbed, and an amalgamation was announced with the Birmingham house of Nettlefolds, known to the outside world for its former association with Mr. Chamberlain. At the same time great reconstruction schemes were begun in the Dowlais works on American lines.

Sir Christopher Furness, another of our iron kings, was over in America in the autumn, and came home with plans for reform. Sir Christopher had already done much, and set about to do more. The Millom and Askam Company has shown what could be done in this country by introducing American blast furnaces, with capacity for enormous output and adequate mechanical appliances for handling the metal. This company, with its new furnaces, has an output of over 2,000 tons a week, as against about 800 tons under the old equipment.

To-day the Consett Iron Company, the Dowlais works, and Bolckow, Vaughan and Co. are all preparing to reconstruct their works, at large expense, to meet the new condition of things. The reconstructions are mostly in the hands of the Philadelphia engineer, Mr. Roberts, and are being carried out on distinctively American lines. The more active firms are getting together, and one of the developments of the future may be a very considerable amalgamation of British houses. For our English iron masters now know that maybe soon, maybe not till a little later, they will have to fight for their very existence. It only needs a dull time in America or a continuance of the present expansion for

England and Europe to be flooded with American iron and steel.

The gravity of American competition was undoubtedly increased by the formation, early last year, of the then billion dollar (£200,000,000) Steel Trust, planned by Mr. Pierpont Morgan, and financed with the support of the Standard Oil group.   The advantages given to American steel production by the formation of this trust were first cheapness of production, secondly a command of the great means of distribution. The Steel Trust is being worked in harmony (not as a combination, but, to use the words of a Standard Oil leader, an " aggregation of interests ") with the American railroad and shipping combine.

The result of the formation of the trust has been to enable the Americans to produce at lower cost than ever before.   The *Iron Age*, a premier trade journal of America, whose name is sufficient guarantee for the accuracy of its editorial statements, specially investigated the question whether the combination had cheapened the cost of production or not.   The facts given by the *Iron Age* were not wholly new, having been to a certain extent revealed earlier by Mr. Schwab, President of the Trust, in his evidence before the U.S. Industrial Commission.   But they are well worth the careful consideration of all enquiring the reasons for American industrial progress.

The method the *Iron Age* found adopted by the United States Steel Corporation was this.   There are in the corporation a considerable number of constituent companies carrying on like manufacturing operations. First of all a uniform system of accounting was developed, to establish a basis for comparison. Meetings were held of the chief accountants of the companies, and by conferences they worked out a system. This preliminary process involved a very large amount of detail work, for the comparisons to be of value had to allow for many agencies that would influence costs. For instance, one plant may have natural gas as fuel, while another is run on manufactured gas. Such differences had to be brought into consideration. Costs were analyzed, and certain basal cost items selected, but especially the relative efficiency of the different plants. Then comparisons were made in competitive sheets, showing the relative strength and weakness of the management of each.

The next step was to see how each company could learn from others doing similar work. Committees were chosen from officers of the constituent companies, the ablest of the superintendents, managers, or men in charge of departments engaged in particular branches of manufacture affected. Those committees studied the cost sheets available, and began a tour of inspection of the different plants in order to observe methods, exchange experience with local managers, or make suggestions. It is their work to find why one can produce at lower cost than another. Frequent conferences, abundant discussion, and free speech are the rules of these committees. They attend to the smallest details, knowing well that it is on the apparently trivial things that the great profits depend.

By all this a standard of cost is fixed, and any manager whose cost of production of particular items exceeds the average is expected to improve till he comes up to the standard. Statements are prepared, showing the various companies what they will gain if they come up to the record of the best. The keenest rivalry is promoted between the different companies, only the rivalry is in this case for mutual benefit rather than for mutual destruction. The *Iron Age* states, as a result of its own investigation, that in one department the attainable cost, based on an average efficiency of a number of the better-managed works, represents a possible saving of £600,000 a year for all companies manufacturing the same product. Much of this saving has since been effected. The managers are educated up to the practice of the most efficient.

" One point is worthy of mention," adds the *Iron Age*, " as bearing on the general question of developing the maximum efficiency of works management, and upon the attainment of a minimum cost of manufacture, and that is, that all the leading men identified with the producing side have an interest in the profits of the concern with which they are identified. The works managers are not simply salaried men. They are practically partners who share in the financial results of the establishment. The putting into practice of the system described has already resulted in economies, which in the aggregate amount to many millions of dollars."

For long there was no more pitiful story in our whole commercial history than that of the South

Wales tin plate trade. In ten years the tin plate trade fell from a gigantic industry to apparently near its end. It had long held the American markets, and seemed secure against all. Then the Americans took up the manufacture themselves. The McKinley tariff gave them an opportunity of which they were not slow to avail themselves. Great mills were erected, fitted with the newest plant, and much money and good brains were put into the business. By 1892 America was turning out 18,000 long tons ; it now averages between three and four hundred thousand tons a year. The British export trade to America was practically destroyed. There is no question here but that we lost much of our trade largely because of the backwardness of our manufacturers. The trade was a profitable one, and, holding a world's supremacy, our manufacturers and men went to sleep. But here again during the past year there has been a decided improvement in methods, and learning from adversity our tin plate makers are entering on a new era.

The American machine tool has triumphed everywhere. You find it now used throughout England. Glasgow itself goes to America for its machine tools, while one of the leading firms of American tool importers, C. Churchill and Co., Ltd., has a branch in Birmingham. Even the Royal Mint has introduced American annealing furnaces. I understand it has found that they increase the output by about fifty per cent., and are much easier and cleaner to manage. At Woolwich Arsenal a large number of American annealing furnaces of one pattern are in use, and more are to come. Our officials do not boast of their purchase of American machinery, for they know that such purchases, if published, mean questions in Parliament, charges of lack of patriotism and the like. But they have to buy, all the same. The American machine tool is now found in practically every progressive English working plant. In Sheffield itself, the home of English tools, the makers are now using American apparatus, working from American patterns, and are paying the American inventors heavy royalties. This should be as alarming to those who know anything of trade conditions as is the other fact, that the American consul at Birmingham frequently receives local inquiries for American makers of such peculiarly Midland articles as cold stamped rivets, builders' ironmongery, and steel butt hinges.

The engineering strike was the real commencement of the introduction of American steel goods into England ; the great cycling boom was the beginning of the introduction of the American automatic tool on a large scale. English firms had to increase their output. Some of them sent to America for machine tools. Others saw these tools, and their use spread here like wildfire. In turret lathes and ordinary lathes the Americans have been especially successful. In the old-time British lathe the workman lost time by substituting one tool for another. In the turret lathe a full selection of tools is fitted in the lathe, and the workman by turning his turret brings the tool he wants into use. To save time is to save money, and so, though the

Americans charge high prices, often demand heavy royalties, and though British workmen and masters by no means care for these new inventions, the stress of competition has forced them to adopt them.

To imagine that this American invasion of our iron trade has been easy, or an unbroken success, would be quite wrong. It has been undertaken in face of great difficulties, and the Americans have had to educate our makers. Wherever the Americans have shown weakness they have been driven back. Let me give one case where England held her own. In the height of the cycling boom a number of American cycles were despatched to this country. But they so differed from the standard patterns here that they were not welcomed. The rims were wood instead of steel, and the tyres single ; the rear fork end was not adjustable ; mudguards, when supplied, were an inch or two too short, and the machines were considered too light for our roads.

The best American makers proceeded to remedy these defects, but their work was largely thrown away by the action of others. Many of the cheaper American machines were rubbishy, and some of the importers were not over scrupulous. Consequently American cycles got a bad name here, and the trade has never recovered. Each year up to last the American imports of cycles were smaller than the last. But perhaps this is also partly due to the fact that the best brains formerly in the American trade have now abandoned that for automobile manufacture.

American bridge competition is typical of the

whole. Ten years ago England was first in this industry: now England is very much second. Here each engineer makes his own patterns, and endeavours to give his designs an individual touch which shall be the distinctive mark of his work. The Americans have standardized their patterns. Their large practice in constructing new ways in the West has enabled them to perfect their plans, and they have fitted up most elaborate bridge-building machinery. They have reduced the work to an exact science, and, thanks to standardization, the putting together of the greatest bridge is like putting together the parts of a Waltham watch. Hence American bridges to-day are cheaper, simpler, better designed, and can be much more rapidly constructed than any we can make.

This was first seen when contracts were asked for the making of Atbara bridge, a structure of 622 tons. The English wanted twenty-six weeks for construction, and asked fifteen guineas a ton. The Americans offered to do the work in fourteen weeks, for £10 13s. 6d. a ton. Our manufacturers complained of favouritism when the Americans got the contract. For the Gokteik Viaduct in Burma the difference was still more striking. This is a much larger work, of 4,332 tons. The Americans asked £15 a ton and one year for construction: the English wanted £26 10s. a ton and three years to complete the work. For the Uganda Viaducts of 7,000 tons the Americans wanted £18 a ton and forty-six weeks' time: the English £21 12s. 6d. and 130 weeks' time. In each case the work was given out under English engineers

—Sir Douglas Fox for Atbara, and Sir A. Rendel for Gokteik and Uganda. If there had been anything like equal competition they and the official authorities over them would naturally have preferred English makers. But even patriotism must draw the line at giving an English maker sixty per cent. more and delaying our work two years while he does his share.

Once the English watch, clock, and instrument maker was among the most skilled handicraftsmen in the world. Then came the American. His goods were so much cheaper that they swept the field. English and Swiss goods alike went down before them. The Americans had spent enormous sums in designing and perfecting the finest machinery for turning out watches on a wholesale scale. Their wares lacked the finish of the English goods, but they were durable and workable. It seemed as though English watchmaking would become one of the lost crafts, and as though our " makers " would be quickly reduced to " jobbers," who find their employment in repairing American and German timepieces when they get out of order.

But the English trade woke up. Our manufacturers put in up-to-date machinery also. Now a big English trade is once more done in home watches. The American and Swiss still hold the field in cheaper lines, both in clocks and watches, but for the better quality articles the English maker is once more to the fore.

CHAPTER VII

THE NEWER INDUSTRIES

ONE of the most serious aspects of the American industrial invasion is that these incomers have acquired control of almost every new industry created during the past fifteen years. In old trades we are hard put to it to hold our own : in the newer we scarce make any pretence of doing so.

What are the chief new features in our modern life ? They are, I take it, the application of electricity to traction and domestic purposes, the telephone, the passenger lift, the typewriter, the automobile, and the multiplication of machine tools.

In each of these, save the petroleum automobile, the American manufacturer is supreme ; in several he is a monopolist. These new industries, be it noted, are enormously profitable. The men they employ are well-paid mechanics, prices rule high, and they form the bases for future advances in industry.

The typewriter affords a striking example of my contention. Machines are brought to England

from New York to the average value of about
£4,000 a week. The cost of the raw material used
in the typewriter is comparatively trivial, and the
greater part of the outlay goes in liberal wages for
skilled labour. The typewriter trade employs and
gives prosperity to whole communities of mechanics in America. Time after time English firms
have attempted to acquire this trade, but in vain.
At present the only serious competitor with the
American machines for office use is a Canadian typewriter.

Why have we failed here ? Chiefly because our
manufacturers have lacked money enough to put
down the proper plant, and partly because we cannot
find here mechanics sufficiently skilled in this particular branch of trade. At first Americans were
protected by their patents, but the main features
in modern machines have now run through their
time of patent protection. The original patents of
the Remington, for instance, have long been public
property.

Every one who knows anything of typewriter
manufacture can recall numerous attempts on this
side to oust the Americans, but all in vain. In one
case an English financier bought the rights of a typewriter for £1,000 and put another £1,000 into the
business, thinking that he could thus cover the
market. The Americans would spend many times
more on a single machine tool in their factories. In
another case the English directors had plenty of
money, but they lacked business skill, and they are
said to have sacrificed £150,000 before they gave

up.   The Typewriter Union in New York, the central organization, which controls the majority of the leading American machines, has a capital of six millions sterling.   Cash registers are another instance of American mechanical ingenuity creating a considerable industry.   The value of the cash registers sent abroad from America last year was nearly a million dollars.

Turning to telephonic instruments, the action of our own General Post Office supplies the best commentary.   The telephone, as all the world knows, was invented abroad, but the earliest practical instruments were made in England.   At first it seemed as though the great business in manufacturing telephonic instruments was to be built up by England.   But improvements were made, and English makers could not obtain the rights to work the best patents.   When the patents ran out the telephone exchanges here were almost altogether, if not wholly, under the control of the National Telephone Company.   This company, doubtless for adequate business reasons, prefers to give its contracts to foreign makers rather than to risk failure on the experimental efforts of the now backward English firms.

Then came the new departure of the Government in commencing active opposition to the National Telephone Company.   There seemed a possibility that the British manufacturers might now have a chance.   Mr. Hanbury, speaking for the General Post Office in the House of Commons, in March, 1899, said : " Hitherto what I believe might be a great trade has gone abroad. I hope that we shall get such competition that the trade for making telephonic instruments and the rest will be established in this country, and that we shall not any longer have to make our purchases abroad."

There seems no doubt but that our postal authorities were really desirous of helping home manufacturers if they could. But on inquiry they found that no English firm had facilities for supplying the large number of instruments wanted in the given time. Moreover the American manufacturers were so much ahead that it would have been foolishness not to buy of them. The central battery switches, for instance, and the apparatus designed to work with them, could not be procured in England, as the Western Electric Company of Chicago held the best patents. Even Government departments, however desirous for patriotic reasons of supporting home workers, cannot afford to stock their works with second-rate apparatus. Within the next few years many million pounds will be spent in this country for telephonic installations and instruments. The money for the instruments will go almost wholly to America or to Northern Continental Europe. English makers are out of it.

But it is in the manufacture of electric material and the promotion and control of electric traction enterprises that the greatest triumphs of the Americans have occurred. When the construction of steam railways opened up a new era in industry England was first, and the rest of the world nowhere. English engineers designed, English

capital financed, and often English labour constructed the great lines of many lands. To-day
steam is hissing its own funeral dirge, and electricity
is rapidly taking its place as the motive power of
the immediate future. How do we stand here ?
There is only one opinion on this matter. England
is to-day right behind in the industrial developments
of electricity.

On this point it is not necessary to produce much
evidence. Let me quote one statement, which in itself should suffice, the verdict of the leading British
electricians themselves. On March 25 last a committee of the Institution of Electrical Engineers,
embracing such names as Professor Perry, Professor
Ayrton, Professor Sylvanus P. Thompson, and Mr.
A. Siemens, drew up a series of resolutions beginning
thus : " Notwithstanding that our countrymen have
been among the first in inventive genius in electrical
science, its development in the United Kingdom is
in a backward condition as compared with other
countries in respect of practical application to the
industrial and social requirements of the nation."

A survey of the trade more than bears this out.
Our great electric contracts are continually going
abroad. The new Central London Railway was
electrically equipped by the General Electric Company of New York, and the same company, through
its English selling branch, did much of the equipment
for the West London electric tramways. The London County Council has done its utmost to keep the
equipment of its tramways in English hands, but
the underground work of the section so far entered

on is in the hands of the London offshoot of the New
York electrical house of J. G. White. The point work
is American, the trucks for the carriages are supplied
by Brill's of Philadelphia, and the ploughs by Messrs.
White. When the London underground railways
were to be transformed there was a long fight as to
whether the system adopted should be American
or Hungarian—British was not thought of.

As one New York technical paper put it not long
since : " For the past few years when any important
English· electrical railway contracts were pending,
it has not been a question as to who, but as to which
American would carry off the prize." Between one-
half and two-thirds of the motors for street cars in
England to-day are American. The Brill Company
of Philadelphia and the Peckham Company of New
York hold the field for trucks, although their monopoly is being threatened by another American
firm—the Maguire Co., which has now established
works in Lancashire. Macartney, McElroy and Co.
of New York boast that they are the contractors to
fourteen British Corporations. The British Thomp-
son-Houston Company, who are the selling agents in
this country for the General Electric Company of
New York, have provided electrical apparatus for
the following street car systems:—Blackpool, Bristol,
Devonport, Dublin United, Dudley, Glasgow, Guern-
sey, Herne Bay Pier, Douglas Southern, Leeds,
Liverpool, London United, Margate and Ramsgate,
Manchester, Middlesboro', Stockton and Thornaby,
North Staffordshire, Nottingham, Portrush, St.
Helen's, Sheffield, Swansea, Brighton, and Rotting-

dean. The London house of Blackwell, which largely acts as selling agents for American makers, has secured a considerable number of contracts throughout the country. The Westinghouse Company, which shares first place in America with the General Electric Company, secured so many contracts here that it has now formed a British Westinghouse company, and erected gigantic works in Lancashire for its European business—works so important that they are separately described later in this book. J. G. White and Co. of London, the English branch of the well-known New York house of the same name, have not been in England very long, but already have secured the Bournemouth Corporation contract, worth £150,000; the conduit work for the London County Council section from Westminster to Tooting, valued at about £171,000; and work in various towns in the provinces. The American houses are finding our field so profitable that they are doing their utmost to become English as quickly as possible. They hold, with some truth, that British corporations would prefer to give their work to be done in England rather than abroad if they could. So they are erecting works here, rushing over American machinery, and in some cases picked American workmen, and are floating English companies.

If English manufacturers have lost their home market, it is not surprising that they have let the foreign and colonial trade go to the Americans. The American engineer to-day is erecting electric plant in Australia and South Africa. The list of great colonial contracts in American hands is too long to be given here. One noted case, the Sydney City and Suburban Tramways, costing ultimately £700,000, was given by the New South Wales Government to America. The first contract was valued at about £160,000. The generators were from the General Electric Company, the piping from Pittsburg, the engines from Milwaukee, the steel for the power house from the American Bridge Company. The Auckland, New Zealand, tramways, and the power plant at Kalgoorlie, are being erected by J. G. White and Co.

The electric business will be perhaps the most gigantic of all in the future, and the capital invested in it will in a few years leave the expenditure on steam railways behind. The money now in our electrical enterprises amounts to £165,000,000.[1] In street traction expansion is going on rapidly. Municipalities in all parts are transforming their tramways to electric power, and there are 2,237 miles of electric lines either constructed or in course of construction in this country. If the industry had a free hand, the number would be multiplied fourfold in fewer years. American capitalists have their agents in London to-day eager for the chance of spending their money in this way on us, for there is hardly an investment safer or more profitable. England, by its compactness, is a land naturally made for this method of transit, and the men of the West know it, if we do not. The short distances between our cities and towns, the great suburbs of our large centres of population, and our many villages, repre-

[1] Garcke's *Manual of Electrical Undertakings*, 1902.

sent, from the traction experts' point of view, mines of untapped wealth.

The Americans have been checked somewhat by the great difficulty of obtaining Parliamentary consent for the construction of new tramways, and by the exclusive policy of many local authorities, which obtain provisional orders for construction, not that they may construct, but in order to prevent outsiders from doing so. But they are not yet at the end of their resources. One of their schemes is to build electric lines along their own roads, as steam railways now are. For some time land has been quietly bought up along picked routes, the promoters estimating that the increased land values made by the opening of the lines will more than repay them, apart from any profit they may get on the electric railways themselves. When these real estate deals are completed Parliament will be asked for powers to construct, and asked with strong local support behind the proposals.

So far, both in this country and America, the business has mainly been confined to laying down electric tramways. Now bigger things are coming. We have the substitution of electricity for steam on the " L " railways in New York, and not only are all our new underground railways in London electric, but the old lines are about to become so. Engineers are already solving the problem of applying electric traction to long-distance trains. The electric monorail, with its swift trains, will before many years be familiar, and the change from steam to electricity for all trains inside London must come in time. This is already done, with much success, at the beautiful Orleans terminus in Paris. It is a sign of the times that the directors of the New York Central Railroad are enquiring into the possibility of transforming their entire motive power from steam to electricity. One of the most gigantic industries of the twentieth century is springing to maturity under our eyes.

In the summer of 1900 there was a Light Railways' Exhibition in the Agricultural Hall, London, where the overwhelming proportion of exhibits was American. Early last autumn a similar Exhibition, on a much larger scale, was held at Madison Square Gardens, in New York City. I had the good fortune to attend both, and at the latter I searched the stalls carefully, hoping to find some evidence of British activity in America, as I had formerly witnessed the American activity here. I could not find the name of a single British firm in the catalogue, or any British goods in the show. Another point struck me. In the Agricultural Hall Exhibition the people present were mainly financiers, municipal authorities, and those at the top of the industry. In New York motor men and mechanics from the neighbouring systems flocked in, and examined the details of the newest inventions and best methods with keen interest. They took intelligent concern in their calling, for they knew, as the English workman does not, that they too might in time come to the top. The President of the Street Railways' Association, the body that was responsible for the exhibition, was himself, when a lad, a mule-car driver in Kansas City. President Vreeland, head of the

Metropolitan system of New York City, began life as driver of a delivery cart and labourer in a gravel pit. The New York car drivers had some reason for their interest, for they knew that what Holmes and Vreeland did they might do too.

One vigorous effort has been made in England to keep our electric trade for ourselves by Dick, Kerr and Co. Splendid factories have been erected at Preston, fitted with the best American machinery, managed at first largely by American engineers, and with Mr. Sydney H. Short, formerly leading spirit in the American Short Electric Company, as Technical Director. The Preston house has undoubtedly done much to revive electric manufacture in England. It has competed successfully for much foreign and colonial trade, and is evident proof of our power to progress if we will.

Why have Americans conquered this big trade ? It is easy hastily to blame English manufacturers, but the fault lies not so much with them as with the legislative restrictions that have hampered electrical work here. The electric industry has been crippled at every turn by many laws, and by the often ridiculous and grandmotherly restrictions of the Board of Trade. Conditions have been made so onerous that most people would not invest their money in it, and those who did found it next to impossible to obtain permission for the initiation of any electric traction or power schemes. Corporations and local authorities have done all in their power absolutely to prohibit developments, and Parliament has backed them. We have all been terribly afraid lest the promoters of new schemes, in benefiting the public, might make large profits for themselves. We laugh at the opposition of our grandfathers to steam railways. Our fight against electric traction is a more foolish example of the same spirit, and we are giving coming generations good cause to scoff at us. While we kept our engineers back, Americans were experimenting. Early electric lines were faulty, but they showed the way to improvements. When in England we were willing to make a small start, we had to go to America for our apparatus. Americans learned in this way to meet the needs of our market. They had the start, and have kept it. Our makers now must force their way against entrenched and secured rivals.

Again I appeal to the statement of the Committee of the Institute of Electrical Engineers. They reported our backwardness to be largely due to the restrictive character of the legislation governing the initiation and development of electric power and traction enterprises. They recommended that the clauses in certain Acts which enable local authorities indefinitely to block local schemes should be repealed, that the Government departments which control the industry should be properly staffed, that the departmental regulations affecting engineering developments should be revised, and that the excessive time and expense needed to obtain permission to carry out electrical developments should be seen to.

These are very modest requests, yet the carrying out of them would give the industry the greatest

possible aid in England. The committee has behind
it the hearty support of every one who knows anything of electric developments. But what hope is
there of obtaining improvements from a Parliament
that is profoundly contemptuous of commerce ? Mr.
Gerald Balfour, President of the Board of Trade,
has, it is true, now advanced so far as to admit that
we are behind, electrically, and that our laws may
have something to do with it.

The Americans are now strong in their position
in the English electrical world. They have secured
so great a reputation that it is becoming quite an
ordinary thing for English local authorities, when
issuing specifications for contracts, to name various
makes of American goods which must be provided.
The British maker, even though he may have improved his products up to the American level, does
not even have a chance to compete. This is as
though the War Office asked for bids for the supply
of pickles, but stipulated that they must be solely
of Heinz's make.

To show this, take the supply of car trucks. As I
said earlier, two American firms have obtained most
of the orders here, orders which are justified by the
undoubted excellence of their output. But now the
local authorities, having learned that the makes
of these two firms are good, refuse in case after case
to consider any others, but declare that Brill's or
Peckham's must be given regardless of rivals.

That I am not over-stating, a few quotations from
recent contracts will show.

The Brighton Corporation, in its tramway con-

tract specifications issued on January 31 last, stipulated : " The trucks are to be of the Peckham
standard cantilever."

In the specifications of the Borough of Croydon
Tramways, dated January, 1902, it was provided :
" Two trucks of Brill or Peckham standard maximum
traction type of the latest pattern are to be supplied
and fitted to each car, and contractors are to send
in with their tenders detailed specification of the
type of truck they propose."

Specification of the Lancaster Corporation Tramways, November, 1901 : " Each car to be mounted
on a Brill or Peckham standard cantilever extension
truck of the following general dimensions, viz. . . . "

Specification of the Sunderland Corporation Tramways, January, 1902 : " Car trucks.—The trucks are
to have a wheel base of 6 ft., with four 30-in. wheels,
and to be of the Brill type, complete with brakes and
equipments, as hereafter specified."

The authorities who prepared these would probably grumble about the backwardness of the British
manufacturer, though they give him no chance.

In the manufacture of automobiles we have
another instance of an industry throttled by over-
legislation. Our makers did not start fair, and it
is little wonder if they for long were not able to
approach their rivals. In automobiles the Americans have done a considerable trade here in two
kinds, the " run-about " or cheap steam motor, and
the electric. One scheme that is now threatening to
displace the old-fashioned London coachman is so
novel that I must refer to it. Mr. Paris Singer, head

of the well-known American sewing machine family, had his attention aroused to the possibility of electric carriages for city use. He spent two years in working out details in America and Europe, and last year began a business in London which is bound to revolutionize our carriage industry. To indulge in horses and carriage in West London is an expensive luxury, the stabling alone often amounting to a few hundred pounds a year. The horses can be had at as high a price as one cares to pay, the carriage needs constant repairs, and coachman and groom, veterinary bills, cost of horses going to grass, and a hundred and one other expenses make the bill one which only a rich man can contemplate with equanimity. And even after all is paid one can obtain but very limited use out of a carriage and pair.

Mr. Singer has set about changing all this. His scheme is to sell automobiles, and then, for a fixed annual charge—about £180 a year—to stable and clean, supply all the power they require, insure against accidents, provide even new tyres and repairs, and, in short, do everything required except supply a driver. The scheme has caught on greatly among rich men, and electric broughams of the Singer type may now be seen in all parts. The Queen and the Rothschilds are among the earliest to take up the new thing, and the electric brougham is rapidly becoming a fashionable fad. Mr. Singer is now spreading his garages over Europe.

In photography the Kodak has swept all before it. The Kodak is manufactured in America, and is sold

by a great American photographic trust. So large a
business in American photographic goods has been
built up that we now import over a million dollars'
worth of them each year. A certain proportion
of these, however, go from here to the Continent.

CHAPTER VIII

LONDON TRANSIT

LONDON was long the scoff of the world for its absence of rapid transit facilities. Of all great capitals, excepting Pekin, it has been the most backward in this matter. The congestion of population, the inconvenient exits and entrances of the old undergrounds, and the total absence of electric traction, made swift movement impossible. Out of the centre of the City, hansoms afford convenient locomotion for the well-to-do ; but they are beyond the reach of the great majority. From Temple Bar to Aldgate even hansoms fail, for they are blocked at every turn by the crush. To this day it remains true that the man who wishes to go from Fetter Lane to, say, Old Street (to mention only one out of many hundred routes), can go quickest by walking.

Other places set London a good example. Even little boroughs like Dover left us behind. Cities of the sleepy East and frontier towns of the far West had facilities beyond our hopes. Until quite recently London did not even attempt to meet the problem. It was ignored. It was left for the Americans to grapple, for they realized, as every student of modern transit knows, that there are mines of wealth here beyond the richest fields of South Africa.

Various efforts were made at times to secure concessions in London transit, but in vain. The old tramway companies were prevented by their legal position from instituting changes. The law took as great precautions to check them giving London a swift service as though to do so were a great crime. Some years ago a South African syndicate offered to buy up the tramways on liberal terms and transform them into an electric service. The County Council, which was then the tramway authority, prevented this.

The London County Council is itself acquiring the tramways in its own radius as they fall in, and is now transforming them. It has already afforded London a striking example of delay. The majority of members of the Council have left the matter to drift, and tramway construction will be for them a time of great trouble. The few interested deliberately educated the local authorities up to obstructing the one method most applicable to outer districts—the overhead wire. They committed the Council to a policy which will involve an expense and an upheaval of the parts affected such as the majority of members have now apparently little idea. The London County Council is going to undergo a rather harsh education on this matter during the next few years, an education which those best acquainted with the admirable work the Council does in many directions can only regret.

The real pioneer of electric traction work in London was Mr. J. Clifton Robinson, who, himself an Englishman, works now largely in association with Mr. Pierpont Morgan. Mr. Robinson took over an old and despised tramway line in the outer Western suburbs of London, and entered into a campaign of education which lasted many years. By the indomitable perseverance of this one man local authorities were conquered, and even Parliament was induced to consent to an electric service for the outer West. If ever the story of Mr. Clifton Robinson's crusade is fully told, it will rank as one of the romances of business. Then came the making of the Central London Railway, where American capital played a large part. The tube system, of which it is only fair to say an English company was the pioneer in the City and South London Railway, caught on, and Parliament granted powers in various directions. Then money became scarce, and it seemed that some of these concessions must lapse. At this point the Americans came in in force and practically took the whole matter out of our hands. The Americans are in two rival groups, the one headed by Mr. C. T. Yerkes, of Chicago, and the other by Mr. Pierpont Morgan.

Mr. Yerkes, creator and long supreme in the transit systems of Chicago, sold out his holdings in that city and early last year settled in London. Mr. Yerkes formed a syndicate, first of American capitalists and then of the Old Colony Trust Company of Boston and the London house of Speyer Brothers. He secured control of the District Rail-

way, and prepared to transform it to an electric
line. Here he was faced by one great difficulty.
The Metropolitan District Railway, which owns
half of the London underground Inner Circle, refused to fall in with Mr. Yerkes. It wanted to adopt
a Hungarian system of electrification—the Ganz—
while Mr. Yerkes wished for an American. The result was a long fight before a special Parliamentary
Committee, for, owing to the close association of
the two lines, it was essential that their method
should be the same. In the end Mr. Yerkes won,
the Parliamentary Committee reporting in his
favour.

Meanwhile he was not idle. The Baker Street and
Waterloo Railway, in course of construction, had
fallen into difficulties owing to the failure of a
notorious group of financiers. He acquired control
of it. The Charing Cross, Euston and Hampstead
line came under him, as did the Brompton and
Piccadilly Railway and the line from the Great
Northern Railway to the Strand. These lines have
yet to be completed. This session various extensions
and a new line were applied for.

Meanwhile the Morgan syndicate was working.
Mr. Morgan has long been deeply interested in the
financial possibilities of electric traction. His group
of supporters prepared a bomb for the Yerkes group
in the shape of a scheme for a line from Ludgate
Hill, past the Temple and Charing Cross, round by
Piccadilly Circus up to Hammersmith Broadway.
This would go right through a large part of the most
profitable territory of the Yerkes group. The Lon-

don United Tramways, the Clifton Robinson promotion, were brought into the scheme.   An alliance
was secured with the City and North-East Suburban
Railway, a line which it is proposed to run from the
Mansion House, past Aldgate, to Victoria Park and
Hackney.   This alliance was secured practically out
of the mouth of Mr. Yerkes.   At the same time
another scheme for a North-Eastern London Railway was pushed forward by the same group.   The
Morgan syndicate agreed to take a half interest in the
London United Electric Railways, the company
formed for the scheme from Hammersmith to
Piccadilly Circus, two-thirds of the capital in the
City and the North-Eastern Suburban, and the whole
in the Piccadilly and City and the North-East London.   The amount of capital necessary can be judged
from the estimate of the engineer, Sir Douglas Fox,
that the cost of construction alone, apart from
electrical equipment, will be £11,000,000.

The war has been hotly fought before a Parliamentary Committee.   The Yerkes group has already
obtained much that it wants, and, although the
Morgan group has failed at some points, great concessions are being acquired by it.   Whether Parliament consents to much or little, the control of internal London transit has definitely passed into
American hands, and the control of internal London
traffic means a profit beyond the dreams of avarice.

CHAPTER IX

THE GENESIS OF THE TOBACCO WAR

THE bold raid of the American Tobacco Company into the British market has excited more attention than any other part of the American invasion, except the conquest of the Atlantic shipping by Mr. Pierpont Morgan.

This raid has come upon us, not because of the supineness of British manufacturers, but because of their activity. The Americans, in their attempt to establish a world-wide tobacco trust, found that the enterprise and triumphs of British manufacturers were everywhere their hindrance. It was this that compelled Mr. James B. Duke, President of the American Tobacco Company, to fight the British companies upon their own ground, and to make a great effort once and for all to crush them. Hence the war, beginning with the purchase of Ogden's at a fancy price, and going on to the combination of British manufacturers and the sensational moves on either side, which have attracted such notice during the past six months.

To understand the campaign we must go back. The struggle for supremacy began over twelve years ago in New York City, when the American Tobacco Company was formed. This great Trust is without question one of the most successful and aggressive of existing trade combinations, headed by one who brings into his campaign the finesse, the foresight, the great plans, and the ruthlessness of a Napoleon. Its resources are almost as great as its ambition. In America manufacturers, jobbers and retail sellers have time after time striven to combine against it. Ordinary law and civil law alike have been appealed to for its suppression. It has had to face vast commercial combinations which appeared irresistible. It has had its temporary checks and seeming defeats, but the end of each year has seen it stronger than at the beginning. To-day it is more powerful and richer than ever before, and in America it controls 95 per cent. of the trade.

On Sunday, October 11, 1899, Major Ginter, head of the well-known firm of Allen and Ginter, then recognized as the premier tobacco house in America, conferred with a young manufacturer, Mr. James B. Duke. Proposals had been made before this that they should join forces. Now definite details were discussed. On the same afternoon the two formally met three other leading makers of cigarettes. Major Ginter, by right of the position of his firm, presided over the gathering; but before the meeting broke up one and all knew that their real leader was young Mr. Duke. He imposed his personality on his former rivals, and he secured for himself better terms than the others had at first proposed to give. It was seen that he was the man to carry things through to a successful end. Then and there the trust was formed, with a capital of $25,000,000, and embracing five leading houses, Goodwin and Co., W. Duke, Sons and Co., W. S. Kimball and Co., Kinney and Co., and Messrs. Allen and Ginter. Duke's received 30 per cent. of the capital, Allen and Ginter 30 per cent., Kinney 20 per cent., Kimball 10 per cent., and Goodwin 10 per cent. " After this agreement had been reached," said Major Ginter in describing the scene, " we all shook hands, and I said ' We are now a company.' "

American public opinion was then strongly opposed to the idea of trusts, and the new tobacco organization studied to keep itself as much from view as possible. Mr. Duke secured the loyalty of the employées of his own firm by distributing among them a number of shares of common stock in the new company.

Other manufacturers were naturally greatly concerned at this combination, and until it knew its own strength the trust sought to conciliate them. Thus Messrs. Duke and Son wrote to one firm stating that the union had been formed for the purpose of buying at first hand from the farmers, and so saving intermediate profits. Again, it was announced that its great work was to be the forcing of American cigarettes on all foreign markets.

Meanwhile the Trust was making ready for its campaign. It determined to fight on clearly marked lines. It had control of the great Bonsack cigarette-making machine, by which as many cigarettes could be manufactured in a day as a man with hand labour could turn out in a month.   Injunctions were sought for against rival machines, and other patents were contested as bitterly and as far as the law would allow.

To capture the public extensive advertising was begun, many of the methods adopted being new. For instance, on one occasion three thousand telegrams were sent to a town in Connecticut authorizing the persons who received them to obtain from any local retailer a packet of the new brand of cigarettes These telegrams cost 1s. 10d. each, but the advertisement was worth it.

When there came the rage for button portraits packets of cigarettes were issued containing coupons for these.   On the introduction of Duke's mixture a fine briar pipe was given with every pound packet sold.   One December 150 Christmas trees, finely decorated, were placed in the windows of various retail cigarette stores.   These were trimmed with ornaments, which were to be given to the consumers of a brand of chewing tobacco then brought out. Art was called to the aid of business.   Splendid pictorial advertisements appeared on the hoardings everywhere, and the newspapers were full of pictures of really admirable quality, all proclaiming the virtues of various tobaccos and cigarettes.

The middlemen or jobbers in the tobacco trade practically controlled the retailers.   The Trust determined to control the jobbers.   By March, 1892, having now felt its feet, it took steps to compel the jobbers to fall into line with it. A contract was submitted to them, which they had the option of agreeing to or else ceasing to deal in their goods on profitable terms. This contract practically changed the jobbers from independent vendors to agents of the Trust. Under it they were forbidden to handle any other tobaccos than those made by the company. No goods were sold outright to them. They received consignments to dispose of on commission. This commission was practically all their reward, and if they were found handling the goods of any other maker they were deprived of the special rebate.

The Trust did not hesitate to penalize those who disobeyed it. One dealer had several brands of his own, some of which were manufactured for him by Kimball and Co., a firm in the Trust, and others by a firm in New Orleans. The Trust ordered this dealer to place the manufacture of all his brands in the hands of the Trust. He declined to do this, whereupon he was offered the choice between immediate obedience or having his supply of cigarettes cut off. It is said that when the company was formed a sum of ten million dollars was placed on one side as a reserve for fighting purposes, to beat down competition and opposition. As soon as a rival company was formed and attempted to do business the Trust never rested until it had absorbed or destroyed it. Rival after rival was bought up. First among them came the National Tobacco works of Louisville, for which £360,000 was paid, a third in cash. About the same time Whitlock's cheroot factory at Richmond was bought up, the price being £60,000, with an annuity of £2,000 a year. The Barby Brothers and Gail and Ax, two of the leading firms in the South, doing business annually between them amounting to £600,000 a year, were secured.

As an illustration of the promptitude of the Trust's methods, within two weeks of the purchase of Whitlock's business it had placed upon the European market Whitlock's Old Virginian cheroots. These, known in the States as " five-center " cigars, were sold in London at five for a shilling, or practically the same price.

Mr. Duke ruthlessly employed a method of getting prices to a minimum in order to advertise his wares or to crush a rival. This was clearly brought out in the evidence given by him not long since before the United States Industrial Commission. Mr. Duke said that to introduce a brand, instead of spending a large amount on bill posters and advertising in newspapers, one plan is to make cheap prices and leave the dealers to do the advertising and work up the market for themselves. Thus " Battle Ax " was introduced and sold for a time for thirteen cents a pound, though the price was subsequently raised to thirty cents. This plan had been adopted before the formation of the Trust by Duke, Sons and Co., who had cut the price of cigarettes very low. In North Carolina " American Beauty " cigarettes were sold last year for $1.50 per thousand, exactly the amount of the revenue tax. As a discount was allowed to the traders this meant that the American Tobacco Company was actually selling cigarettes for nothing and paying the purchasers for taking them. "That is only one of the methods followed in order to gain the victory," said Mr. Duke. "After the goods are put in the store you have to rely on the public as to whether you have made something that the public is satisfied with or not. No matter what the inducements are the quality must sell them, and there is nobody who can stop an article from selling when there is quality in the goods. . . . We take care of the public all right because they are our customers, and we feel just as much interest in every consumer as we do in the dealer. We are not making any schemes to get the dealer. The consumer is the man we want, and through the consumer we get the retailer and the jobber also. We give tags and all other inducements we can, as well as the best goods we can, in order to get them to use our goods."

Naturally the methods of the Trust and their purpose to secure domination of the trade aroused intense opposition. The most serious form this assumed was the establishment of the National Cigar and Tobacco Company, with a capital of £500,000, and, as was subsequently stated, with a million of reserve to be drawn from as occasion demanded. Its fighting brand was known as the "Admiral" cigarette, which was advertised largely, and was keenly in demand by the public. The retailers would have it, and called in the jobbers to purchase it. This placed the jobbers in a peculiar position, for the Trust notified them individually that if they handled the new cigarette or had any dealings with the new company they would lose the commission already due to them and their supplies of the A.T.C.'s goods would be cut off. As the A.T.C. was at this time (1893) making and selling 98 per cent. of the cigarettes consumed in the States, it will be understood that the jobbers could not well afford to defy it.

Those of the jobbers who did handle the "Admiral" cigarettes, to please their customers, found that they could now obtain the Trust's goods only at prices which meant loss to them. Vans attempted surreptitiously to deliver in the depths of the night, but nothing could escape the sleuth hounds of the sleepless Trust. The jobbers had to give in.

Then the National Company rose to the occasion. As its goods could not be delivered in the ordinary way it would undertake to distribute to the retailers itself. As a paper at the time expressed it, " They made up their minds to be in at the death when the Trust had finished its fight. They had invested two and a half millions of dollars in a concern of a manufacture protected by law, and they did not propose to show the white feather while their cash held out." Twenty-five delivery wagons day by day carried goods from the company's premises to the retail dealers in New York, and deliveries were arranged for in all the great cities in the country.

At first the National Company seemed likely to succeed. Thus one large dealer in Broadway declared his independence. As usual the Trust announced that unless he ceased to stock " Admiral " cigarettes it would not sell him its goods. He refused to yield, and here the Trust had to give way, attempting to save its dignity by announcing that in this particular case it would make a concession.

The hope of the National Company lay in the fact that they had purchased for fifteen years the control of the Elliot cigarette machine, which was said to be equal, if not superior, to the Bonsack machine used in the Trust factories. The Trust did all in its power to prevent the rival company using this machine. It invoked the aid of the law, and when judgment was given against it it appealed again and again, alleging that its patent had been infringed. It carried the case from court to court, until the highest tribunal was reached, and in the end it was defeated.

This was apparently one of its recognized methods of warfare.

In the spring of 1896 the National Company carried the war into the enemies' camp. On evidence supplied the directors of the Trust were indicted by the Grand Jury in New York on a charge of conspiracy to control the price of paper cigarettes. The case, which attracted considerable attention, dragged on for several months. In February, 1897, certain charges were sustained by the Judge of the Court of General Session. These charges comprised a conspiracy to coerce and compel all wholesale dealers to sell cigarettes at an arbitrarily fixed price, and refusing to supply those who sold below such prices ; to coerce and compel wholesale dealers to deal exclusively in the Trust's cigarettes, by unlawful aggression, and also by such agreement to fix and control the production, manufacture, and output of cigarettes. Of course such prosecutions had little ultimate result.

The National Company scored point after point. In 1896–97 it was said to be running twenty-one of the Baron cigarette machines, with an annual output of 100,000,000 cigarettes. It advertised largely on the lines of the Trust, and offered many prizes, including one of $1,500, to be run for at the Jockey Club track at New York. Coupons for this were included in every packet of cigarettes. It also gave away with its five-cent packets jewellery estimated by outside people to be fully equal to the price charged for the cigarettes. The Trust answered move with move, and the advertising attractions of its rivals were met by it. The demand for cigarettes went up by leaps and bounds.

A trade paper, *Tobacco Leaf*, gave a graphic picture of the fight about this time. "For a period of three years the commercial world has been within sound of a mighty conflict waged for supremacy between the National Tobacco Company and the American Tobacco Trust. On both sides an efficiency of generalship has been displayed which, if expended in the massing of armed men, would long have commanded the admiration of the world, for if the one side has its Wellington the other has its Bonaparte. The responsibility for the National Company rests with Sigmund Rosenwald, its vice-president, while J. B. Duke commands in the camp of the American Tobacco Combination. In the arts of strategy the two men are about equal. To an outsider it seems as if they occupied identical positions

in regard to the confidence of the opulent corporations each upholds. Whatever they do passes un-
challenged by those about them. Their word is law.
To a considerable extent both Duke and Rosenwald
are men of like temperament. They both know
they are right, and go ahead. They do not stand in
awe of each other. Each appears as if he were face
to face with doughty foes. It has been my fortune
to hear them complimenting each other at long
range, with reserve and reflection, trying somewhat
to justify their rival courses. In my conversation
with the two kings of tobacco I became impressed
with the notion that Duke is the more austere. His
thoughts of the progress of the fight never leave him.
He evidently takes his business problems to bed
with him. Rosenwald, on the contrary, while never
neglectful of business, loses it when he puts on his
evening clothes. Their ability to despatch and
accelerate business is about equal. Perhaps Duke
is the better model of method, but what Rosenwald
lacks in quality he makes good in nervous energy."

What was the end of this great battle ? It can
be related in a few words. At the end of October,
1898, Mr. Bernhard Baron, who had been the prime
mover and a large shareholder in the National
Company, told a representative of the English paper
Tobacco the story. For some years they had tried
with all the money necessary at their command to
gain a foothold in every conceivable way and to
obtain the patronage of the American public. The
" Admiral " cigarette had been advertised in every
corner of the United States, and money had been

lavished in many directions to get hold of the trade of the public, but without success. All the time the American Tobacco Company grew more and more powerful. "The American Tobacco Company's great stronghold in America," he said, " is the public, both the masses and the classes ; and, controlling and buying as they do from sixty to seventy per cent. of the bright tobaccos of Virginia and North Carolina, they are in a position to give the American public the best article for the least money, which they can do as well if not better than any one else. It is safe to say that any organization, even with a capital of $50,000,000, would not affect the American Tobacco Company in the least, and especially under the presidency of Mr. Duke, whose ability has brought the company to its present high standing. As long as he lives and is at its head it is sure to progress, and will be the greatest concern that the world has ever seen."

This was said when a new combination, the Union Tobacco Company, was being formed, with a capital of £2,000,000, to fight the Trust. Mr. Baron thought such a fight an impossibility, and to oppose the Trust, with its prestige, financial standing and splendid management, was a waste of time, money and energy.

The policy of boycotting rivals was nominally abandoned by the Trust a few years ago, but its opponents maintain that this is still done. Before the Industrial Commission Mr. Hugh Campbell, president of a rival concern, the United States Tobacco Company of Richmond, Virginia, positively stated

that the Continental Tobacco Company, the associate
of the American Tobacco Company, which manufactures, owns and controls the brands of between eighty
and ninety per cent. of the tobacco sold in New England, went to the jobbers and promised them a discount of three per cent. if they would handle their
goods to the exclusion of others. Finding that this
was insufficient, the Continental Tobacco Company on
January 1, 1901, reduced the ordinary discount from
two cents per pound to one cent, but raised the
extra discount of those who refused to handle independent goods to five and a half per cent.

Mr. Campbell further said : " The Trust refused to
sell jobbers goods, not because there was a question
of credit at all, but simply and only because they
persisted in handling independent goods. That has
had a deterring effect on others. They have been
held up as a warning to all who might be inclined
to go and do likewise ; and to-day, and for the last
twelve months, there has been a ' reign of terror ' in
New England. Dealers are afraid to sell as they
would like to do goods that they have bought and
paid for." In answer to a question why he did not
obtain a remedy for this under the Anti-Trust Law,
Mr. Campbell said it would be impossible, he thought,
to get voluntary evidence, as purchasers would
suffer. " It would be too expensive a business for
us to go to law with a corporation of this magnitude,"
he said. " One company tried it for years, and they
are out of existence to-day. The National Tobacco
Company carried on suits for years in New Jersey
against the American Tobacco Company, and they

were carried over year after year, at least for a long time. If they failed with all the capital they had behind them it would be pretentious for a little concern like us to make such an attack."

This charge of boycotting was emphatically denied by Mr. Duke. " Well," he said, " I do not know what the agents have done, but they have not done anything of that kind with the authority of the company ; and I do not believe they have done it, because if the jobber handles another fellow's goods that does not make a market for them. I think every jobber in New England is handling other goods besides ours. . . . There never was any agreement to the effect that parties handling our goods should not handle the goods of other manufacturers—nothing except at one time they got a larger commission from us if they did handle ours exclusively than if they did not. That policy was abandoned four or five years ago."

But evidence was further given by various tobacco dealers, showing that they had been offered special discounts by the Trust if they would refuse to handle the goods of competing firms, and then, when they refused this, the Continental Tobacco Company had declined to do business with them or supply them at all with its goods.

Meanwhile the Trust was waging another war. It entered the plug tobacco business in 1895, and came into direct opposition with the great St. Louis firms, chief of which were Leggett and Myers, whose factories occupied a frontage of a mile. The Trust brought out a new brand of plug tobacco, and advertised it in the newspapers and by posters as never had tobacco been advertised before. The St. Louis manufacturers united, and announced to the retailers that as the Trust had struck at their plug trade they in turn would strike at the special trade of the Trust. They brought out a cheap line of their own in plug tobacco, and made preparations also to fight for cigarettes. Within a few days of the Trust entering the plug business representatives of nine of the leading manufacturers met at the Planters' Hall, St. Louis, to organize their campaign.

This was not an opposition to be ignored. Mr. Duke announced that there would be no further dividend that year on the common stock of the American Tobacco Company, as profits would be kept for buying up new plants and businesses. The Trust never borrows money. This sent American Tobacco Company stock down with a rush, and in a few hours it had fallen from 79 to 70, and then down to 67$\frac{1}{8}$. In April, 1897, a declaration was received from the Circuit Court at Chicago that the American Tobacco Company's attempt to control the cigarette trade was illegal, and prohibiting the Trust from doing business in the State of Illinois. The same judgment declared that the Trust was a monopoly, and as such a menace to commercial integrity.

But the triumphs of its enemies were short lived, and 1898 was for the Trust its great year of victory. Firm after firm in the second or third rank disappeared. Three of the big independent houses—

Brown, T. C. Drummond and Co., and Mayo and
Bolton—were secured. Organized opposition was for
the time broken, but Leggett and Myers, in many
ways the greatest firm of all, refused to capitulate.
Its president announced that he would never have
any dealings with the Trust while breath remained
in his body. The Trust in 1899 engineered the
formation of a subsidiary company controlling the
plug interests it had acquired.

A third great rival, the United Tobacco Company,
was started by a former secretary of the Trust, and
was practically a split from it. But this opposition
was bought out. The president of Leggett and
Myers sold his stock and retired in disgust. In
April, 1899, the American Tobacco Company increased its capital by £7,000,000, and took over
entirely the United Company, and at one stroke
amalgamated all separate houses, and opposition
was destroyed. With the absorption of the United
Tobacco Company organized attempts to stem the
tide of success of the Trust were for the time broken
up. It is worth noting that Mr. Duke is reported
to have said that eight per cent. could be guaranteed
from the beginning on the capital of the new scheme.

The Trust had captured the cigar trade, and
now practically had the American tobacco in its
hands.

It would be a mistake to suppose that the great
Trust has even now all its own way in America.
Rivals are constantly cropping up, but the fight
is usually like that of a pigmy against a giant,
for the Trust has its agencies everywhere. It

can largely control purchases of the supply of
the leaf, and it does things on such a scale, and
backed by such resources, that its opponents stand
little chance.

CHAPTER X

MR. DUKE in due course felt himself strong enough to attempt the conquest of the world. His two great companies—the American Tobacco Company, with a capital of £16,000,000, and the Continental Tobacco Company, formed at the end of 1898 with a capital of £20,000,000—were the two wings of his army. These two companies though nominally separate were really one, Mr. Duke being the president of both, and some of the directors directors in the two. The main work of the American Tobacco Company was manufacturing all forms of tobacco except cigars and plug, and the Continental Tobacco Company made plug and smoking mixture. Early in 1902 the nominal separation between the two was broken down and they were openly controlled by a new combine of the Consolidated Tobacco Company. The companies have for some years been earning profits which enable them to maintain long and costly wars. The American Tobacco Company had net earnings in 1900 of £1,260,000, and in 1901 of £1,329,000.

After paying its dividends early in 1902 it had a surplus of £1,276,000, and assets valued at £18,236,000. The Continental Tobacco Company earned in 1900 £896,000, and in 1901 £1,520,000. It had a surplus at the end of 1901 of £918,000, and assets amounting to £22,324,000. It is worth noting that seven millions of the assets of the American Tobacco Company consist of stock in other commercial concerns and in foreign investments.

The Trust, with this income behind it, was in a position to plan great campaigns, and Mr. Duke was sighing for other lands to conquer. He negotiated for the tobacco monopoly in Japan. He had striven hard to acquire the entire trade in France. He bought up a great company in Germany, and by his negotiations struck terror into the hearts of manufacturers in Russia. His representatives went on tours round the world, seeing what countries were worth snapping up. He had a long fight in Australia, where in August, 1894, a company was established under the name of the American Tobacco Company of New South Wales, with a capital of £60,000, and with the sole rights of the Bonsack and Bawn machines in New South Wales and Queensland. One company of prominent manufacturers was brought in. About the same time similar companies were formed in New Zealand, Victoria and South Australia. The Trust had already established itself in South Africa, and in 1895 despatched a representative to Johannesburg to establish a cigarette factory there.

This however did not flourish, owing to the heavy duties on cigarettes and free import of the leaf.

The first great battle in Australia was strangely enough with a firm which afterwards was to be sucked into the Trust. Ogden's was then a British house, sounding the patriotic cry for all it was worth. Its advertisements continually urged the British public to support British industry by buying British goods. National symbols, from the Union Jack onwards, were frequent in its announcements. It had an exceedingly clever advertising manager, who knew how to strike this national note to the full. In 1899 Ogden's "Guinea Gold" cigarettes had a hard fight with the Trust's brands "Vanity Fair" and "Duke's Cameos," and there was a fierce struggle for supremacy.

The one country where Mr. Duke for long could do nothing was England. Here he positively lost trade, and in a hundred foreign fields his agents found themselves baffled by the activity of the agents of the great British houses. The American Tobacco Company had settled in England. It had an office at Holborn Viaduct, and on the occasion of the Budget of 1898 it made a special effort to secure the British trade. But American cigarettes made no headway here. Mr. Duke himself, who rarely takes the public into his confidence, was compelled by the United States Industrial Commission to give the world a peep behind the scenes. In his evidence before this body, which is so far as I am aware the only recent public statement he has personally made, he said : " We find our chief competitors abroad in cigarettes from England mainly. They buy our tobaccos in North Carolina and Virginia, ship it over there, manufacture cigarettes, and then compete with us in all the foreign markets. That is true of tobaccos as well as of cigarettes. Of course there is limited trade in tobacco in the other countries as compared with here."

Question : " But England is your chief competitor ? "

Answer : " Yes. A few years ago England did not do much in the line of cigarettes, but now there are large manufacturers in England, and they use New Carolina and Virginia tobacco. We have lost trade in Great Britain ; we will have to establish factories in England. The duty discriminates against manufactured tobacco. In other words, you can import the leaf there, and pay the duty on it, and manufacture the cigarettes at a total cost of from forty to fifty cents less per thousand than manufactured cigarettes can be exported there from this country. They discriminate against the manufactured article to that extent. The only means of getting into that market is to establish our own factories there and pay the same duty as the British importers do."

This declaration was soon followed by actual developments. In the autumn of 1901 Mr. Duke came to England and bought up the British firm of Ogden's. This house, with an ordinary share capital of £100,000, paying ten per cent., and £200,000 of preference shares at five and a half per cent., was purchased for the very high price of £818,000. In excusing the sale the chairman of the company said that the Trust had set aside £6,000,000 to conquer Europe, and if Ogden's did not sell out it would be beaten. The Trust at the same time announced that it would set up its own factories for cigarette making in this country, so saving the extra duty it had up to then to pay on imported cigarettes.

Mr. Duke entered into negotiations with other British firms. It is said that he offered the English house of Wills £9,000,000 for its business ; but the offer was refused. Seriously alarmed, the principal manufacturers prepared to meet their rivals. They sank minor differences, amalgamated their forces, and early in 1902 floated themselves under the name of the Imperial Tobacco Company, with a capital of £15,000,000, of which just on £12,000,000 was paid in cash, shares and debentures to the thirteen firms which formed the combination. Of this Messrs. Wills received £6,992,223.

At first everything seemed in favour of the British combination. Public sympathy was undoubtedly strongly with it, and the retail traders, alarmed by accounts of the methods of the American Trust in other lands, favoured the British concern. The British company had the retail trade of the country almost wholly in its hands. Its brands were well known and popular, far above those of the rival Trust. It seemed that the Napoleon of the tobacco trade had at last met his Waterloo.

By a series of extraordinary moves the British

combine largely threw away its advantages and played into the hands of its opponents. Its first mistake was the purchase of the great retail firm of Salmon and Gluckstein, the shares of that company being turned into ten per cent. preference shares of the new company. Salmon and Gluckstein were a very enterprising house which, by cutting profits to a minimum, had secured prosperity for themselves and had inflicted heavy loss on the old retailers. Their branches had been established in a few years almost everywhere in England, and they were hated by the rest of the trade to a degree which it is hard for the outside public to realize. By purchasing the business of Salmon and Gluckstein the Imperial Company largely alienated the general body of retailers.

This might have been overcome, but a second and worse mistake followed. At the time of the amalgamation the British company had promised the retailers a substantial bonus. No details were given, but the retail trade was led to understand that it would very largely benefit. The announcement of the terms of the bonus was delayed for many months, the reason apparently being that the Imperial Company in the first rush of public enthusiasm became somewhat too confident of its strength, and thought that the steps it had first contemplated for conciliating the retailers were now unnecessary.

The announcement of the terms of the bonus was made on March 18 in a circular issued broadcast amongst the trade. The Imperial Company stated that it had set apart a sum of £50,000 for the first half-yearly distribution, and that subsequently a bonus equal to one-fifth of the profits of the Imperial Company on their home trade, after their debenture and preference shareholders had been paid their dividends, would be given. But in order to benefit by this agreement the tobacconists were required to sign an agreement which absolutely bound them not to buy stock or sell in proprietary goods manufactured or sold by the American Tobacco Company or by others objected to by the Imperial Company, in writing. Mr. Duke's representatives were not slow to see the handle this gave them. " This is a boycott pure and simple," they said, " and is a new element introduced by the Imperial Company into the trade. It is specially stated to be directed against ourselves, but it is a dangerous weapon to place in the hands of the Imperial Company, as apart from ourselves it enables them to debar you from purchasing goods from any person, company or firm they may object to. They may object to your purchasing from any one but themselves, and you will remember that by Clause 2 you have to conform to their prices and terms from time to time. This is a serious question for retailers, as it would enable the Imperial Company practically to make their shops into tied houses, which would be carried on for the benefit of the Imperial Company."

The day after the Imperial offer was announced Mr. Duke made a bid, which by its astounding audacity fairly took away the breath of the British traders. He agreed to give the trade customers of Ogden's the entire net profit earned by the company (of course the British company, not the old American concern) and £200,000 per annum as well for the next four years.

The Imperial Company replied by modifying its first agreement. It again circularized the trade, stating that while for the purpose of protection it reserved to itself the power prohibiting the sale of certain goods by those receiving the bonus, it had no intention of exercising its power in an arbitrary or unreasonable manner. It now offered to allow recipients of its bonus to stock the American Trust goods so long as they did not display them in their windows.

It further called its customers' attention to the attempts of the American Tobacco Company elsewhere to boycott rivals. "We have hitherto anticipated," it stated, "that Mr. Duke intends, if he ever obtains the power, to exclude the goods of his competitors. In this day's newspaper we find the following paragraph as illustrating the policy of the American Tobacco Company, which deserves the attention of retailers as well as manufacturers :—

" 'From Ottawa it is reported that the representatives of the tobacco manufacturers of Ontario and Quebec will meet the members of the Canadian Government to-day and ask for intervention against the American Tobacco Company.

" 'The American Tobacco Company bought up the Empire Company, a Canadian company using Canadian leaf, and is now enforcing a contract agreement upon all wholesale grocers and tobacconists, compelling them to refuse to handle any tobacco

made of Canadian native leaf except that manufactured by the Empire Company, under the threat,
if they refused to comply, of the American Tobacco
Company refusing to supply them with any brands
of American tobacco.'

"It now appears, however, that Ogden's, Limited
(the American Company's organization in England)
come forward as advocates of unfettered trade, and
in assuming this part they have put forward a
perverted view of our bonus scheme."

But the British company had the worst of it, and
knew it. The Americans were now before the public
in the light of the defenders of free trade: the British
as advocates of a policy of boycotting. The public
sympathy which the Imperial Company had received
up to this point now largely left it. The retail trade,
too, rose in rebellion, and almost wholly refused to
sign the agreement. " The Imperial Company,"
said one retailer representing his fellows, " has out-
Americanized the Americans." And the retailers
saw that behind the bonus systems of both trusts was
the intention of the wholesalers to get the retail trade
entirely in their power, and this they determined
they would not permit.

While, however, the Imperial Tobacco Company
has injured itself at home, it has been active abroad.
In foreign fields it has done better. In America in
particular it is carrying the war into the enemies'
country. There it has formed an alliance with the
United States Tobacco Company, headed by Mr. J.
P. Butler, who was formerly in the Trust.

The struggle has led to a very great increase in

tobacco advertising in the newspapers and to the reduction in price of various packet cigarettes in this country. Some of the evening papers have been obliged at times to double their editions, displaying their tobacco advertisements. Thus in one day both the *Star* and the *Evening News* of London were enlarged to eight pages for this purpose, and the *Evening News* received £400 for its advertisement. Packets of cigarettes which formerly fetched fivepence now go for threepence. The fight promises to be a long one.

CHAPTER XI

COAL

BRITISH supremacy in the world's coal trade seemed for long absolutely indisputable. This country produced the largest quantity of coal of any nation, and our hard coal was considered so far the best in the world's markets that British merchants would scarcely discuss the possibility of competition. To-day our supremacy has gone. The United States is now the greatest coal producer, and American anthracite is rivalling our own in quality and price in the great foreign centres.

During the latter half of 1899, when the price of coal was artificially and very considerably raised in this country, the industrial combinations that control the Eastern American coal trade cast their eyes on Europe to see if they could not take some of our export business from us. They were heavily handicapped by their great distance from European markets, and English mine owners at first thought it absurd for them to dream of fighting us. But there were points in their favour which gave the Americans a growing advantage. Their coal is much easier to extract than ours. Owing to the rapid growth of mining in this country, our seams are ever getting smaller, deeper, and more difficult to work. America, on the contrary, has to tap practically virgin seams, often almost on the hill-side itself. America uses coal-cutting machinery more largely than we do, and this means a considerable reduction in the cost per ton of bringing to the pit mouth. The appliances for handling are more elaborate across the Atlantic than here, and enable the shipping of the coal to be done at a lower rate.

The lowering of the Atlantic freights coming then, the Americans found themselves able to put coal on the markets at prices which for the first time made competition possible. Sample cargoes were consigned to various European ports, but at first there was very great difficulty in getting them tried. The British held the field, and in commerce as elsewhere the man in possession has many advantages. After a time small orders were obtained, and despite the failure of some cargoes, it was found that the quality of the American product would bear comparison with our own. Some favoured the one, some the other. Many merchants condemned the American coal for its friability. Others became enthusiastic over it because, they said, it had a smaller percentage of ash. But, as the British Consul at Marseilles has said, " Americans have been able to get their coal on the market, and this alone has considerably modified things in their favour. American seam coal has been tried and found to be in quality far superior to expectation. The old prejudice is beginning to disappear. The difference in firing value between British and competing American qualities, hitherto estimated at ten per cent. in favour of the British, has already come down to seven per cent. Americans hope before long to be able to convince their customers in the Mediterranean by practical experience that the difference in results is solely due to European ignorance in the handling and firing of their coals. Indeed, they have already succeeded in doing this to an appreciable extent during 1901. . . . The first step has thus been successfully taken."

At Marseilles the American coal imports increased from a very small amount in 1899 to about 200,000 tons in 1901. The P.L.M. Railway and the Cie. Générale Transatlantique gave large contracts. But the lowering of British prices in the autumn of 1901 injured the American imports, and if the English prices went down a little more, and Americans remained as they are, there would be little hope for the Americans. This state of affairs, however, is not likely to arise. The British prices may, and probably will, go down, but fresh factors will arise on the American side.

In Germany the Americans came sharply into competition with the German industrial combinations. The Stettin firm of Stevenson imported the first lot into the country, and made a mistake in the kind selected. Then Herr Schulze, the well-known Berlin buyer, who had hitherto patronized England, went over to the Americans. " I intend to get rid of all the British coal I have in my docks, and trade solely in American coal," said Herr Schulze to a correspondent of the *New York Coal Trades Journal* last December. "German manufacturers, dealers and large consumers whom I have been supplying with Welsh coal are eager for American hard coal. That is where the future of America's hard coal market lies. The Reading coal is harder than the Welsh, and therefore affords more heat and power. The drawback with ashes will soon be overcome by chemical experiments now being made. I have ordered another 10,000 tons in addition to my first order of 10,000 tons, and have an option of another 10,000 tons with the Reading Company. Moreover, I am satisfied that arrangements will soon be consummated by which we will obtain special advantages in transportation charges, and facilities from Philadelphia. Heretofore the big coal mine operators of Pennsylvania have not paid much attention to our markets because they seemed busy supplying home demands. I found that the question was not ' How much does it cost ? ' but ' How much can I get ? ' But the opportunities which now present themselves for the complete revolution of the German hard coal trade in favour of the American product are such that they cannot be longer ignored."

In Germany American coal is not having all its own way. Many complaints are being heard of it, and it has not cleared the field yet. But the striking fact is that it should be selling in Germany at all. In Switzerland American coal has now secured a sure foothold, largely at the expense of German.

During 1901 Atlantic freight rates touched their minimum, and this greatly strengthened the hand of the coal kings.   It was possible to send coal from Philadelphia to Bordeaux for 5s. a ton, and many cargoes went from the Eastern States of America to Hamburg for 5s. 6d. a ton.   These prices were of course quite exceptional.   But the Americans have been maturing a scheme for making their rates even lower still.   They propose to build fleets of very large coal steamers of 10,000 tons each, and to use them for capturing the European trade.   Had the Shipping Subsidies Bill been carried through Congress this spring, these steamers would have been laid down, and the competition of America in our Mediterranean trade would have been more serious than ever before.   Now that the Subsidies Bill has been shelved, such steamers may be run by American capital under the British flag.

In the fight for the world's coal trade the Americans have everything increasingly in their favour. England and Germany, to-day their main competitors, have failing mines.   In this country a Royal Commission is now sitting, inquiring, among other things, into the length of our possible coal supply.   It is not likely that our coal will in an appreciable time be exhausted, but every day makes it more probable that it will be so much more difficult and costly to obtain as to be unable to hold its own.   The same is true of Germany.   America, on the contrary, has scarcely touched her resources.

Within a generation we may see American coal brought to England, as American iron is now being done. To some the possibility may seem absurd, but it is certainly not so absurd as would have been the forecast seven years ago that we should import American pig iron.

CHAPTER XII

MERELY DOMESTIC

NOWHERE perhaps is the American invasion of our everyday life more apparent, or seen to greater advantage, than in our domestic life. American manufactures and products are commonly used in every English household every day in the year.

Most of the inventions that have tended to simplify the labours of the housewife in recent years have come from America. There servants are scarce, independent and dear. Even before Mr. Sheldon started his recent crusade they did not forget to tell you, "I am a lady, and expect to be treated as such." Rather than stand the ways of the "hired girl," most American housewives of the same standing as those who would here have at least two maids, have elected to take the advice of sturdy old William Cobbett, and do without servants altogether.

This has led to the multiplication of all kinds of devices to save household labour, to the great comfort of the women folk. The American sewing machine might once have been quoted as a case in point ; but though we still import a million dollars' worth of machines each year, the Germans have so taken this up that it can no longer be looked on as peculiarly American. Darning machines, patching apparatus, and a hundred and one other Yankee " notions," now to be seen in every draper's shop, belong to this class.

Automatic carpet sweepers are worth mention. It took long to popularize them here. Our housewives would not realize for some time that with a carpet sweeper they can do in five minutes, without dust, the same work that would take them thirty minutes with a broom, and fill the room with dust. At first, too, carpet sweepers were dear. But in time prices were reduced, and the use of sweepers spread. No housekeeper who once used the sweeper would ever think of replacing it by the broom. During the past three years the American carpet sweepers have sold here by tens of thousands, and every year this sale increases. The business will be a permanent one, for sweepers, like ordinary brooms, want frequent renewal. We buy nearly a quarter of all the American brooms and brushes sent abroad.

Shirt waists, or blouses, as they are called in England, could a year ago have been quoted as an instance of great American success. They cannot now, for British and German merchants, who formerly held this business, have redoubled their energies, and have taken the trade back from America. Yet the temporary conquest of this business was striking.

For many years every visitor to New York remarked on the smarter appearance of even the
poorer women there than their English sisters.
This was largely due to the superiority of the cheap
American blouses. About 1898 some firms in the
Eastern States obtained a few orders for these from
English drapery houses. The shirt waist met with
so great a welcome that in the following year
moderately large orders were placed. These orders
were found all too small, and in 1900 the greater
part of the English ready-made blouse trade went
to America. One English firm alone is said to have
sold American blouses for women to the value of
£57,000. This figure, however, is difficult to verify,
and those most familiar with the trade doubt its
correctness. But the triumph of the American
trade was undoubted, and it was accomplished notwithstanding many blunders on the part of the
American manufacturers. The trade came to them
too easily, and they would not put themselves out
for it. They refused to look at small orders, and
would only do business with the largest jobbers.
They did not study the English needs. In 1901
the success of the former year was not repeated.
Large orders were given in advance, but by a sudden
change in fashion the striped shirt waist which the
Americans produced was no longer to the fore.
The favourite costume for ladies then was a light,
almost transparent, muslin. This the Americans
were not prepared to supply.

English wholesale dealers frankly admitted the
cause of the temporary triumph of the American

shirt waist. They said that the method of manufacture in the two countries is so different that the
English product must be reformed if it is to stand
any chance whatever. In England the system has
been for the blouses to be roughly cut in factories,
and then given out to home workers, mostly in city
slums, to produce them as best they might, one set
of people doing the whole work on a mass of blouses.
The American plan is quite different. There the
blouse maker brings all his workers into the factory,
and may employ two, three, or four thousand hands.
The cut is more exact, the models more scientific,
and the fit and style better. And in specializing
in the details of making, labour is saved.

At the very first it was found that while for style
the English were behind, the material of the product
in this country was much better than that of the
cheaper American. There soon came trouble, too,
about the price of the American shirt waist. It
was too expensive, the great demand here being
for a medium-priced article. This the Americans,
save under exceptional conditions, could not produce, owing to the heavy duties they have to pay
in importing material into the United States.
They made a desperate attempt to secure the cheaper
market, and over-reached themselves in doing so.
They gave us an article at the right price, but
it was far from being the right article. There was
cut and style and finish, but those who were unfortunate enough to buy these shirt waists found the
first time they had the necessity of washing them
that all the colours ran, and the blouse was spoilt

and made useless. This has practically put an end to the American business here in this article.

Turning to an allied product, the Americans transformed our corset trade. The straight-front corsets which swept the British market last year were an American idea, and at first were very largely manufactured in America. English retailers took them up as an experiment, and they at once achieved a great success. Thereupon some of the most prominent English manufacturers went to school with the Americans. They attentively studied the American makes, adopted the same principles, and to-day are fighting the Americans here on their own ground. But English retailers state that there is still one thing in which American corsets are superior, and it would be well for English manufacturers to take note of this. The American corset has three laces instead of one, thus allowing it to be adapted to any figure without discomfort or inconvenience.

The difficulty of the American manufacturers is to produce goods of this kind at low enough prices for our market. The very cheap German wares undercut them, and, despite all labour-saving machinery, it has yet to be seen that in articles of attire they will have great victories. In men's shirts they will come in if our British shirt-makers do not adopt the two American points of removable cuffs and quarter-size collars. The advantages of these are self-evident to any who have tried the American product. Our great drapery houses are now adopting the American style of window dressing.

The methods of publicity adopted by such houses as Wanamaker's of Philadelphia and New York are bound to win their way here. Wanamaker's have no hesitation in adopting any European idea, and their agents are constantly at work in many lands, searching for smart notions and bright points. The general manager of their house in Philadelphia tells me that perhaps the greatest factor in their continued success—apart of course from the quality of their goods—has been the care they had given to securing attractive publicity. Those familiar with the Wanamaker advertisements in American papers can well understand this. To compare these announcements, and the announcements of other great American dry-goods houses with the heavy and stodgy advertisements of the leading London drapery firms, is like comparing a delicately-carved statuette with a block of rough marble.

In domestic medicine the invaders have inflicted pecuniary loss on both doctors and chemists, not to speak of wholesale drug manufacturers. The Americans have exploited the medicine trade, both legitimate and quack, in the most thorough fashion. We spend £4,000 a week on American patent medicines, made in America and imported into this country. But this is by no means the whole. Many of the chief firms have set up their own factories here, and the trade in patent American drugs manufactured in this country probably very largely exceeds the import trade.

On this let me quote a talk I had with a busy London chemist. " Every year sees the rapid

spread of American drugs in our business," said he.
" In my own case, about half the medicines I sell
are American, and a considerable proportion of the
remainder German. But my proportion is larger
than the average, as there are many American
visitors in this part of London. Taking the trade
as a whole, I should say that one-third is in American
lines.

" Why is this ? Simply because the Americans
are right up-to-date, while our own manufacturers
seem to be asleep. They provide the things wanted
in such a convenient form that the older preparations stand no chance beside them. Here, for
instance, is a box "—and he showed me a little fat
leather pocket-case—" containing all the ordinary
medicines and opiates that a traveller in uncivilized
lands wants, done up in tabloid form. It only takes
up a few inches of room. The old-fashioned English
medicine case, containing the same preparations in
liquid form, was quite a load. Here is another
little leather case for a doctor to put in front of his
bicycle. All of these are American. I sell large
numbers of them. If I wished, I could not sell
similar English goods in their place, for there are
none.

" In new preparations the Germans have rather
got the lead, but for drugs, on the whole, the Americans come first. We did not welcome their arrival.
For us the profit on a bottle of tabloids is much
smaller than it would be on the ordinary mixture.
The only benefit we have is the saving of time taken
in preparation. Doctors were still more opposed to

tabloids, for they take the whole mystery from medicine, and enable a patient to dabble in drugging himself. But they have come in spite of us, and they are here to stay."

Of household foods, corn, canned meat, and tinned fruits, which come to us from America, it is hardly necessary to speak here. The coming of these is no new thing, and enormous as are the quantities of food stuffs sent to us across the Atlantic, we can have no hope of improvement until our farmers are Americanized. But it may be news to some that many of the so-called English foodstuffs, which are sold as home produce, are wholly American-made. I do not state this on my own authority, but on the word of the American consuls, who have repeatedly complained in their official reports of the great amount of canned goods sent unmarked from the States and here decorated with English labels.

In domestic furniture the invasion has not yet really begun, and if the Americans do not hurry they will find that the advances of the English trade have taken the field from them. American manu-facturers have been too busy up to now supplying their own markets to cater for us, save in expensive goods such as office fittings. But the English cheap-furniture market was long waiting for the first progressive firm which chose to annex it. Here our furniture is still largely made by hand by "little masters" in Shoreditch and Bethnal Green, who work with the most primitive tools, who have no capital, and who are at the mercy of the wholesale buyers. Every middle-class and working-class housewife can tell of the rubbish, showy-looking, but rotten, now sold here under the name of furniture.

Contrast this stuff with the cheaper, finer-made, and more durable goods sold all through America and in Northern Germany. These goods, machine-made in great factories on a large scale, would as surely win the day here as American desks have swept away the old heavy British writing tables. But here the English makers are at last stirring. They were hampered for a long time by serious differences with their workmen, and more than one effort to introduce modern American machinery and factory methods failed. But now one big house in East London, which manufactures the best furniture for a leading West End firm, has its factories full of the most up-to-date American inventions. It is true that these machines are mostly worked not by Englishmen, but by Germans. News reaches me that another English company is erecting a big factory in North London, and is also importing a large amount of the best American electrically-driven wood-working apparatus. It is going to adopt American methods right through, and under good management should score a real success. This is only one of the many signs that we are learning to use the weapons of our rivals against themselves, and that in the end the invasion may prove in some ways a blessing in disguise.

Even in pickles and sauces one Pittsburg firm, Messrs. Heinz, has recently covered the English market. Its preparations are to-day to be seen

in half our restaurants and in practically every
grocer's in the country. A year or two since a
firm of soda-water fountain makers, Messrs. Styles,
set up in the City of London. It has now planted
soda-water fountains in innumerable chemists'
shops all over the country, greatly to the comfort
of ordinary folk. An attempt was made some time
back to place American ice-creams on the London
market, the famous New York house of Horton
starting a branch here for that purpose. But it did
not succeed. The British public is not yet educated
up to the ice-cream habit. In fact, with all due
respect to it, it hardly knows what ice-creams are.
The English girl nibbles at a morsel or two of an
indifferent frozen concoction, while her American
sister will devour a plateful or two of the most
delicious cream preparation. The American ice-
cream must come here, and is likely to come soon.

Then even in hotels we find American proprietors
now planning London branches, and if half the
rumours floating around are true, London is likely,
within the next year or two, to see replicas of some
of the most famous New York houses here. It is
said that the Astor Estate is willing to put five
million dollars in an attempt to run a London copy
of the Waldorf-Astoria.

Talking of the Astor Estate reminds one of the
way in which some great American millionaires are
quietly investing in London land. One central district
has been transformed during the past few years, and
great streets of office buildings put up on it. These
office buildings are run under the names of various

land companies, but there is good reason to believe
that these land companies, or the best of them, are
simply other names for the wealth of one of the oldest
and richest millionaires of New York City.

And recently a syndicate, led by Americans, made
strenuous efforts to buy the finest site in London—
the great block at the bottom of the new Holborn-
Strand Avenue, for the erection of gigantic office
buildings, as much a sky scraper as London civic
regulations would allow.

In the domestic life we have almost got to this.
The average citizen wakes in the morning at the
sound of an American alarum clock ; rises from his
New England sheets, and shaves with his New York
soap, and a Yankee safety razor.   He pulls on a pair
of Boston boots over his socks from West Carolina,
fastens his Connecticut braces, slips his Waterbury
watch into his pocket and sits down to breakfast.
Then he congratulates his wife on the way her Illinois
straight - front corset sets off her Massachusetts
blouse, and begins to tackle his breakfast, at which
he eats bread made from prairie flour (possibly
doctored on the special establishment on the Lakes),
tinned oysters from Baltimore, and a little Kansas
City bacon, while his wife plays with a slice of
Chicago ox tongue.   The children are given Quaker
oats.

Concurrently he reads his morning paper, set
up by American machines, printed with American
ink, by American presses, on American paper, edited
possibly by a smart journalist from New York City,
and sub-edited with as close an approach to American

brevity and verve as English pressmen can achieve, advertising its American edition of some classical novels or gigantic encyclopaedia, which is distributed among the subscribers on the American instalment system.

Rising from his breakfast table the citizen rushes out, catches an electric tram made in New York, to Shepherds Bush, where he gets into a Yankee elevator, which takes him on to the American-fitted railway to the city. At his office of course everything is American. He sits on a Nebraskan swivel chair, before a Michigan roll-top desk, writes his letters on a Syracuse typewriter, signing them with a New York fountain pen, and drying them with a blotting sheet from New England. The letter copies are put away in files manufactured in Grand Rapids.

At lunch time he hastily swallows some cold roast beef that comes from the Mid-West cow, and flavours it with Pittsburg pickles, followed by a few Delaware tinned peaches, and then soothes his mind with a couple of Virginian cigarettes.

When evening comes he seeks relaxation at the latest Adelphi melodrama or Drury Lane startler, both made in America, or goes to a more frivolous theatre, controlled by the great American Trust, where he hears the latest American musical comedy, acted by young ladies and thin men with pronounced nasal accents. For relief he drinks a cocktail or some Californian wine, and finishes up with a couple of " little liver pills," made in America.

CHAPTER XIII

In the railway world American competition and American ideas have during the past year received very serious consideration in England. For this there are obvious reasons. Our railways, after a long period of prosperity, are under a cloud. Their dividends have remarkably declined. New competitors are arising, as for instance inter-urban electrical tramways, depriving them of part of their revenue. Labour becomes steadily dearer. Fuel bids on the whole to show an average rise rather than a fall, and unless some fresh factors arise the position of the British railway shareholder in coming years cannot be a happy one.

Contrasted with American railways ours come out in some ways unfavourably. Our companies have for years adopted a system of charging their main improvements to capital account, and spending their profits in dividends. Hence they have been burdened with an ever-enlarged capital for which to provide interest. American railways on the contrary have largely charged their improvements to current expenses. Thus the Pennsylvanian Railroad, according to its last report, spent for betterments in 1901 over £2,400,000, and in three years the Lackawanna Railway has spent £1,230,000. While our railways are, so far as handling their passenger traffic is concerned, equal to any, they are much behind the Americans in their goods traffic.

The handling of goods by many of the great English lines in an open scandal. Prices are high, delays are constant, and with railways of the second grade it is much worse than with the main lines. It is to-day true that it costs more to send goods from Sheffield to Liverpool than from Liverpool to New York. Twenty years ago it cost English and American railways practically the same to carry goods. The American railways steadily improved: the English stood still. To-day the average rate of working expenses per ton mile on the great American lines is ·36d. per mile. On English lines it is 1·2d. per mile. This has tended severely to injure our manufacturing industries.

It is doubtless true that English railways have in the past been greatly hampered, as they are to-day, by their supreme authority being placed in the hands of amateurs. The control of railways is in itself a profession demanding absolute concentration by the men at the head. In this country it is universal to place supreme control in the hands of the directors, the majority of whom only give part of their time to this work, and have lacked training in the matter. Men are chosen railway

L

directors in England to-day for any reason except
expert railway knowledge. If they are members
of Parliament, and so can help to influence railway
legislation, they are deemed desirable parties.
Now a man may obviously have been in his time
an excellent officer in the Guards, and may make
an admirable member of Parliament, and he may
further do his duties as a county magistrate to
perfection. But none of these things especially
qualifies him for being one of a small body having
the final voice in the control of a great railway.
Yet the qualifications of an English railway director
are usually on these lines, and the real experts
in British railway management—experts in many
ways equal to those of any lands—are under these
directors, and have to submit to them. The most
enterprising General Manager in England may
possibly do a little in the way of reform, but if
he does not carry his Board with him he has to
curb his activity or resign.

Yet English railway authorities have not been
asleep to the possibilities of learning from America.
Last year several of our railway companies, notably
the London and South-Western and the North
Eastern, sent expert officials to America to investigate and report. These officials could only em-
phasize the facts already well known, that by the
use of larger freight cars, by economy in employment of men, and by employing heavier and
more powerful engines for freight, it would be
possible to reduce operating expenses. At a meeting of the North Eastern Railway held last February

Sir Joseph Pease, the chairman, said, "On this matter I am not disclosing a secret when I say that our General Manager and engineer have returned from America much impressed with what they saw, and with a frank admiration for American railroad working, especially in the department of goods and mineral carrying. The results of the visit will, we believe, have fulfilled the expectations of the Board. Our larger engines might have larger trucks and larger loads attached to them with commendable advantage to the traffic expenses."

Mr. Angus Sinclair, editor of *Locomotive Engineering* of New York, a leading authority on the matter, put the advantages of the American system clearly to me in a conversation I had with him last October. After pointing out the lower expenses of the goods traffic in America he said :—

"Why is this? It is not because labour is cheaper in America. On the contrary, wages on the New York Central, to take one leading American line, are said to average nearly twice as much as on your London and North-Western. The main causes of the American economy are the heavier loads drawn, the reduction of dead weight, and the larger freight cars. The English goods wagon is made to hold from eight to twenty tons: the American freight car carries fifty tons. We load our cars to their full capacity: you only half and quarter load many of your trucks. The net result is that while in English goods traffic two-thirds of the weight hauled is dead weight, trucks and cars,

and only one-third paying goods, in America the
proportion is reversed, two-thirds being remunerative.

" The British system is to have a truck at each
little station, and load it up with the goods from
there. Thus a train going from Aberdeen to Glasgow, for instance, would couple on many trucks at
various points, many of them with only one ton
or even half a ton of goods on them. On a freight
train going through from New York to Chicago,
instead of a car being coupled at each station, all
the goods would be loaded on one car till that one
was full ; then a second would be attached, and
so on.

" This economy of freight cars has another advantage. In England great expense is incurred in
shunting the rows of goods wagons : in America
this is avoided. America, too, has nothing to
correspond to the long death list on English railways through coupling by hand. But you seem
quite indifferent to that. In the States the railroads are everywhere required to have automatic
couplers.

" Economy is obtained on American lines by
having much heavier freight trains. Recently I
read an account of a meeting of English engine-
drivers protesting against the increased loads
being put on their trains. ' Why,' one of them
said, ' the companies will soon be wanting us to
have trains carrying fifteen hundred tons.' He
did not know that in America the ordinary freight
train carries far more than that. Five hundred

tons is a fair average on an English line : some Americans take 3,500 tons.

"This point has impressed many of the English managers who have been over here, and they declared their intention of constructing bigger goods wagons and adopting heavier loads.

"Some of the economy of the American lines is doubtless due to the better training of the engine drivers. In England a lad starts as a cleaner, goes on to stoker, and then in time becomes engine driver. Here in America he has to undergo regular and severe examinations before he takes charge of an engine. He has to understand his engine, not merely by the knowledge he can pick up on the line, but in a scientific manner. He has to know how temporarily to repair it in case of a breakdown. He has to master the theory as well as the practice of getting the best work out of it in the easiest way. The American engine driver is ahead.

"If an American manager took control of a British line, probably one of the first things he would do would be greatly to reduce the amount of labour. By your methods many more men are required than with us.

"Old-fashioned equipment and unwillingness to throw on one side the second best locomotives and cars are hindering England to-day. And your rigid road beds involve greater strain and expense than the elastic road beds of the American railways."

Yet it must be admitted that it is to-day no

easy thing for our railways largely to adopt American methods. The employment of heavier locomotives and of trucks on the American plan, carrying four times the present load, might not mean any large reconstruction of our road beds, but it would mean larger goods yards, greater facilities to load and unload goods, and fresh warehouses. In many cases the warehouses not only of the companies but of their customers would have to be reconstructed. A process involving a very large expenditure of capital would have to go on, and while the process would doubtless in the end prove remunerative, yet it would mean the sinking of so much capital that it is not unnatural for our directors to hesitate.

The improved railways of America have beyond question been one of the greatest factors in the industrial growth of that country. " There is no doubt," said the *New York Journal of Commerce* recently, " that the revolution in railroad equipment and construction which has been going on during the past decade has been a vital factor in the competition of the United States with other producing nations. The increase in the amount of freight carried per car and per train, carrying with it the decrease in the ratio of dead weight friction and expenses, has added by so much to the ability of American manufacturers and exporters to compete with their rivals. In just the same manner as the reduction in the rate of interest on money by improvement in our banking currency would diminish the net cost of laying down goods in a competitive market, so the reduction in the cost of carriage has given a corresponding margin of profit or of competitive power to the American exporter."

The competition between English and American locomotive builders has excited much attention. For long our great houses such as Dubs and Co., Neilson, Reid and Co., Sharp, Stewart and Co., Peacock, Byers and Co. and Kitson and Co. largely held the world's market. Within recent years however the enormous increase in the demand for locomotives encouraged the growth of other firms. Two American houses, Baldwin & Co. and later the American Locomotive Company, owner of the Schenectady Works, proved formidable competitors. Large numbers of orders from South Africa, India, Egypt, China and elsewhere have gone to these firms, orders which otherwise would have come to England. The Baldwin Company during the past five years built and exported the following locomotives. In 1896 they built 547 and exported 289. In 1897 501 were built and 205 exported. In 1898 755 were built and 348 exported ; in 1899 901 built and 375 exported ; in 1900 1217 built and 363 exported. The American locomotive came even into this country, where it was adopted by the Midland, Great Eastern, and other railways, because they could not obtain sufficiently quick supplies from the British firms to meet their own demands.

For some time there was much doubt as to the comparative merits of the American and British engines. In price it was easy to ascertain that the Americans, where their standard patterns were adopted, were about 20 per cent. cheaper than the English, although where engines had to be built to special designs they were considerably dearer. But the cost of running and the results of working were not clearly brought out until in June, 1901, the Midland Railway authorities made an important statement through the London *Daily Mail*. The Superintendent of the locomotive department of the Midland Railway, Mr. S. W. Johnson, said that in 1899 they had put on their line thirty Baldwin and ten Schenectady engines, and in January, 1900, a six months' comparative test was made between these Americans and the standard Midland goods engines of British make. The result of these experiments went to show that while the American engines worked their trains satisfactorily, they consumed from 20 to 25 per cent. more fuel, 50 per cent. more oil, and cost 60 per cent. more in repairs. The Midland authorities stated that it would not be correct to say that the American engines are no good, for, although they cost more in working, the conditions under which they have to work in America are different, and these engines were on the American pattern.

These results were supported by various reports that came in later from other parts. Perhaps the most conclusive of them was the official statement made by Lord Cromer concerning the locomotives on the Egyptian State railways. Lord Cromer stated that the Commissioners of the Debt in Egypt insisted on orders for locomotives being put out to competition amongst firms irrespective of nationality. The railway authorities however determined to ascertain by experiments which locomotives paid the better. In the question of price there was a marked difference. Where the British asked £2,240 and £3,250 for locomotives built to design and specifications prepared by the Egyptian Railroad Board, the Americans wanted £2,700 and £3,575 respectively for the same. Where however certain modifications of design were permitted, the Americans offered to supply the engines for £1,855 and £2,475. The reason of this cheapness of the Americans in the latter case was that they were able to introduce stock standards.

In time of delivery the Americans scored. The British makers asked 48 and 90 weeks respectively for delivery. The Americans offered to deliver in 18 and 35 weeks if the Egyptian designs were followed, or in 12 and 30 weeks if the changes they had proposed were allowed. At one time, when locomotives were urgently required, the builders of the Baldwin offered twenty engines in twelve weeks, while the shortest time offered by the European firm was 48 weeks. The result was that the Americans got the order.

The Egyptian railway authorities found that the American engine differed comparatively little from the British as regards quality of material and workmanship, although in some of the less essential parts the work is very rough, and there is a notable want of finish in the American engines. No details could be given about the consumption of oil or cost of maintenance, although the work so far as it had gone seemed to point to the fact that the American would not last so long, and would engage the workshops more than the British.

The special value of the test was on the relative consumption of coal. These tests were personally conducted, and the results jointly signed by a representative sent out by the American builders and the Locomotive Inspector of the Egyptian Railways Administration. Trials were made with both goods and passenger engines. It was found that in the case of goods engines the American consumed 25·4 per cent. more than the British engines, while the latter was drawing 14·2 per cent. more load. In the case of passenger engines the American used 50 per cent. more than the British consumption on the same average load. This latter difference represented, at 34s. 2d. per ton, the average price paid, an additional cost of £400 per annum. The result of experiments in many parts of the world during the past two years has been on the whole favourable to British makers. But, despite this, it is plain that British makers are bound in the future to lose a great deal of the trade. The absence of standardization in this country and the slowness of construction compel foreign buyers to go more and more to the American houses, where they can quickly obtain what they want.

Messrs. Burnham, Williams and Co., of Philadelphia, the makers of the Baldwin locomotive, write to me as follows :—

" It is obvious that the same weight of locomotive, whether British or American, gives the same amount of adhesion, and therefore that of two engines having the same weight on driving wheels, both will haul the same load if properly constructed. It is obvious also that the same boiler pressure in two engines will generate the same power, provided there is no difference in the adjustment of the valve motion controlling the distribution of steam in the cylinders. It is obvious also that the various metals used in locomotive construction such as steel, iron, copper, bràss, etc., have precisely the same qualities whether fabricated in England or in America.

" The difference between the locomotives is largely therefore one of railroad practice. The American engine is designed to give a higher mean effective pressure in the cylinders, and therefore to use more steam in running a given distance, but per contra to haul a greater load, because greater load means greater revenue. English locomotives are generally designed to cut off the admission of steam to the cylinders for economy, and therefore to give less power, and to haul lighter loads with less fuel consumption.

" Americans, and those who have used American locomotives, are satisfied with the economy of the American practice from a broad point of view. Those who use English locomotives, and adhere to English views as to locomotive practice, are satisfied that the English locomotive is a more economical machine, from the narrow standpoint of cost of operating the machine itself, without reference to the work performed.

" It is a fact that few, if any, of the English railways or English-managed railways abroad keep their records in such a manner as to show the cost of operation per ton mile. They nearly always use train mile units, which ignore differences of load in each train. American railroad records are almost invariably kept upon the ton mile basis, which gives a complete index of the work performed, exclusive only of the grades over which the loads are hauled. This is however a large subject, which would require an extensive article to treat it adequately. We have endeavoured merely to touch upon the merits of the case as they appear to us."

CHAPTER XIV

THE WESTINGHOUSE WORKS

THE building of the great works of the Westing-house Company at Trafford Park, near Manchester, is the most important for British industry. It has aroused both masters and men here to the folly of some of our old methods of limiting labour, and has shown what British workmen can do when properly led.

I am indebted to Mr. D. N. Dunlop, of the Westing-house Company, for the following account :—

"It is now a little over two years since the Westing-house Company found that its business in this country had become so important as to necessitate the establishment of special works on the spot. After considerable delay in searching for a suit-able spot, Trafford Park, Manchester, was selected for the great manufactory of electrical apparatus, and the work was begun.

"The spot is almost an ideal one—in the thick of the vast industrial life of the north, with the Manchester Ship Canal and the Bridgewater Canal hard by, and several lines of important railway in close attendance. The works are on a scale that almost baffles the imagination which tries to follow the description of them, and to realize what the figures mean. One hundred and thirty acres of ground have been acquired for this large undertaking. The machine shop alone covers eight acres. The works proper are located in six main buildings, each adapted to one special branch of the industry. There is, first, the great iron foundry ; next to it a small brass foundry ; next the malleable iron foundry ; the pattern shop, which is fireproof throughout ; the steel foundry ; and the forge. The machine shop, 430 feet wide by 900 feet long, is the largest engineering shop in the United Kingdom. The office building, which has a frontage of 250 feet, has, it is hardly necessary to say, every modern convenience, all the latest in the way of heating, lighting and ventilation—in short, it is fitted out on the newest and most approved American lines. Fifteen miles of railroad serve to connect the buildings on the estate, and there is one mile of underground tunnel in which will be placed the steam pipes, and the electric wires conveying current to the motors. In the machine shop alone there will be over three miles of line shafting, with pulleys on the same for driving the various machines. Six million feet of lumber have been used in the construction of the machine shop, and 3,000,000 in the roofing and flooring of other buildings. There are 10,000,000 bricks and 17,000 tons of steel in the various buildings. There are 300,000 feet of skylight glass, with wire woven into the centre of the glass, so that in case of breakage no glass can fall down and injure the employées. Small condensation gutters have been fixed to the underside of the skylights, to gather the condensed water and prevent dripping into the building. At the south end of the shops is to stand a water and electric-light tower which at night will illuminate the entire surrounding district. To paint the entire buildings 100 tons of paint will be required, a figure which conveys nothing to the imagination until we compare it with the thirty-three tons which were required to paint the Forth Bridge.

" The brain reels at the thought of so many figures, and we have doubtless said enough to give the reader, whose interests are not wholly statistical, some idea of the magnitude of the undertaking. It remains to be said that every sort of provision is made, not only for the work, but also for the 6,000 workmen to be employed. The employées are provided with washstands, and lockers in which they may stow their outdoor clothes while at work, and special provision is made for the workwomen employed. The Trafford Park Dwellings Company, an independent association, has acquired land in the Park for the erection of cottages for their own workmen. The cottages are to be lit with electric light, heated with gas —in short, in the home as well as in the factory the workman is to be provided with every comfort that progress has hitherto made possible only for longer purses.

" We have said enough to show in the making an industry far beyond anything hitherto attempted, or even dreamed of, in this country. But the most remarkable fact of all is the way in which the buildings have been completed. When the foundations were laid, in the spring of 1901, it was estimated that some years would be required to complete the building operations alone, and the relation that estimates bear to realization in this country are generally lamentable to the last degree. The company, moreover, were in no mood to waste time and their shareholders' capital in long-drawn-out preliminaries. They engaged Mr. James C. Stewart, of St. Louis, Pittsburg and New Orleans, as building manager; and Mr. Stewart, with half a dozen young assistants from his side of the water, produced with home labour results that are absolutely unique in the records of British industry. In the huge framework of steel pillars, stanchions and girders, 10,000,000 bricks have been laid in record time. The number of bricks which it has been stated the British labourer can and will lay in a day—the number, that is, which his sovereign inclination, backed by the Union, to which all the most respectable workmen belong, will allow him to lay—has proved a fruitful subject of controversy in the periodical press of late. To be more exact, the average of 450 bricks per day has been taken as an established economic fact, and as the basis for unfavourable comparisons, not only with the working capacity of other nations, but with our own achievements in the past. Trade-Unionism is, of course, the scapegoat, but since Trade Unions are a force that has come to stay, the inferiority of the British workman was duly accepted and deplored, and the British 'ca-canny' methods have become proverbial. Almost the first hint we have had that the responsibility for such results lies at the masters' door, comes from a workman who has seen both sides of the question. The masters, according to this authority, have initiated the go-easy methods by their own slackness, and are the sinners, as they are the sufferers, for having allowed affairs to come to such a state. The hint is more than borne out by the achievements of the West-inghouse building manager with British material. While the periodical press has harped on the 450 bricks a day, and the inherent inferiority of the British workman, Mr. Stewart has established an average of 1,800 bricks per man in a nine hours' day, with a maximum of 2,500 for the plainest work. The completion of the buildings as they stand to-day is the irrefragable answer to detractors of all descriptions and nationalities. Whatever means were employed—and there is no doubt that Mr. Stewart left no legitimate device untried—it is certain that these were at least human. Daily reports from all the foremen and sub-foremen were received by the manager. During the third week of operations the average had risen to 900 bricks per man per day, and, by the continuous weeding out of the useless and the idle, the high standard of 1,800 was gradually approached. The Trade Unions naturally did not suffer in silence, and once or twice it looked as if trouble might be pending. In every case, however, matters were settled without recourse to unpleasant proceedings. Managers and delegates met amicably enough and the officials of the Company, with that strength of purpose and energy, the want of which, in the British employer of the last two generations, the workman critic so much deplores, made it perfectly clear that while they would pay not only the Union rate, but an even higher wage than the Union required—11d. an hour instead of 10d.—they meant to manage their own business, and would not be dictated to by the leaders of the Union. If these terms were not acceptable they could dispense with the good offices of the Union and employ other men. The result was peace with honour.

" Every kind of labour-saving appliance was used on the works, perhaps the most remarkable being a monster automatic rivetting machine which strikes 1,500 blows per minute, while the average done by the hand-rivetter is 200 blows. Even to this improvement the British workman took kindly enough when his first suspicions had been allayed.

" It is remarkable that there was no bullying or harrying of the workmen. But also there was no wasting of time, none of that loafing, smoking and conversing which is said to be so dear to the heart of the British workman. The men—3,758 of them altogether—worked for all they were worth. The materials, too, were largely of home production. The timber, of course, was imported from America, but the bricks were made at home—the facebricks came from Accrington, and the terra-cotta work from Doulton's. The steel was supplied by a Middlesborough firm, though the builders tell us it could have been imported more cheaply from the United States. The window frames were ordered from an American firm, and provide an example of the spirit in which business is done on the other side of the water—within eight weeks of the giving of the order some of the windows were already built into the brick walls.

" The building stands completed, and the work of installation is proceeding. The power to work the machinery will be electricity. Steam engines will be in use at first, but it is proposed in the course of two years to substitute the more economical gas-engine for the steam. While the building was going on a number of young British engineers in the employ of the Company were sent to the machine shops at Pittsburg for further training. A leading northern daily waves away with scorn the ' damaging and humiliating' inference that British engineers have anything to learn in the United States. The reason for sending out these men is that they may familiarize themselves with ' the peculiarities of American machine-shop practice' and 'with the methods and ideas which, if not better than our own, are different, and have to be studied on the spot.'

" We may clothe the facts in what language we choose. It is obvious that these methods and ideas, different from our own, have produced on British soil, and with British material, triumphs of workmanship which have not hitherto been obtained by any methods known to British business men.   The organizing ability of Mr. Stewart brought out, as no one had ever done before, what stuff there was in the British workman. *But the stuff was there :* herein lies our great hope for the future, our triumphant answer to the pessimist. Our workmen, under proper supervision, have shown themselves equal to a quantity and quality of work which, according to our detractors, could be found only on the other side of the Atlantic. What has been done so far can, must, and will be done again in other departments. The erection of the huge buildings constitutes a record for speed so far as this country is concerned, and would be a remarkable feat anywhere. In these buildings the manufacture of electrical apparatus, the great industry of the future, will be carried on on lines new to us, though successfully tried in the United States, and the genius which has already achieved such remarkable results cannot fail to revolutionize industry in this country. This British enterprise marks the beginning of a new era—the era of rehabilitation and return to that great place in the world's history of effort and achievement, which we were in danger of losing for ever."

CHAPTER XV

BOOKS AND PUBLISHING

A FEW years ago American bookmen took their tone almost wholly from London. The greater part of American literature was a more or less weak imitation of current English fashion, and Sydney Smith's sneer, " Who reads an American book ? " had still some force. To-day we are approaching the stage when it seems that the London literary world will sit at the feet of Chicago and New York.

The activity of Americans in the book world has led to several marked results :—

The creation of a distinctively American literature,

The forcing up of sales to a point rarely known before,

The employment of general shops (departmental stores) as book-distributing agencies,

The extension of circulating libraries on novel lines.

The creation of a distinctively American literature is no longer a matter of doubt. The American novel has obtained a commercial success in America which the highest work of English writers has failed to command. For instance, a book like *The Crisis* sells in the United States three or four copies for every one of a masterpiece by Kipling. The newer American books are setting a fashion in literature. The novel of business, after the manner of Mr. Robert Barr's racy works, and the novel of politics, are to a certain extent displacing the novel of mere sentiment. And in both the novel of business and the novel of politics the Americans are leading.

In England the sale of 100,000 copies for a novel is considered phenomenal. Across the Atlantic at least one story, *David Harum*, has gone well over the half million. According to figures published in the American *Review of Reviews* last November, there were six novels published there in 1901 which ran into a circulation of 150,000. The actual returns from the publisher's own statement of the sales up to last autumn were :—

David Harum	520,000	copies
Richard Carvel	420,000	,,
The Crisis	320,000	,,
Janice Meredity ..	275,000	,,
Eben Holden	265,000	,,
Quincy Adams, Sawyer ..	200,000	,,
D'ri and I	100,000	,,
To Have and to Hold	285,000	,,
The Christian	200,000	,,
The Eternal City	100,000	,,
An English Woman's Love Letters	250,000	,,
Black Rock } Together nearly *The Sky Pilot*	500,000	,,

The success of American publishing methods is bound, for commercial reasons alone, to bring about their adoption on this side. This change is made the more certain because we have reached a stage in England when book publishing must be revolutionized. Increasing royalties to authors, advance payments on royalties, and the rise of literary agents have done no good to it as a business. The publisher must adopt new methods or go under.

The time has come for a change, and it seems probable that this change will be made on American lines. What are these lines? Formerly publishing there as here was a cautious, conservative business. Then smart men from the West came in, and some of the oldest business houses found that the competition of these new rivals was cutting the ground from under their feet. Harper's had to be reconstructed. Appleton's went into the hands of a receiver. Men like Colonel Harvey Mr. S. S. McClure and Mr. Doubleday took the game in hand, and things began to hum.

Colonel Harvey is a quiet, but very smart editor. He made his mark as a newspaper man on one of the most progressive newspapers in New York City; then he took to finance, and made a fortune with street railways. With money at his back (it is generally understood that the ubiquitous Mr. Pierpont Morgan stood behind him) he took over control of the old house of Harper's, and their machines have since been insufficient to cope with the new business. Mr. McClure is one of the greatest hustlers in America. A single incident will sufficiently show the kind of man he is. Some time ago he came on a visit to England, reached Southampton in the morning, hurried up to London, did a heavy day's work in his offices off the Strand, boarded the evening train at Liverpool, working all the way, and then caught another boat back to New York. They reported recently that he was down with nervous prostration. But that is a minor detail.

The new publishing methods have left behind the old ideas of dignity and restraint in literature. Books are treated not as sacrosanct pages, for distant veneration, but as business goods to be pushed in a business way. A book is advertised after the fashion of a patent pill. As one angry author put it, " The publisher to-day has adopted the methods of the seller of three-dollar boots, and of the boomer of the circus." Even the largest houses have adopted the newest methods.

The use of departmental stores has been one of the strongest planks of the newer American publishing. Mr. John Wanamaker is the largest buyer of books of any retailer in the country. A hundred other great storekeepers in every large city do their best to run him close. Books are given the most prominent display on the ground floor of the big stores. People are obliged to see them, for it is recognized that to see is the first step towards buying. In England this change is slowly coming in. We have not yet reached the stage where Peter Robinson and Jay stock the est novels along with the newest fashions, but it is coming, and the large co-operative stores in west London during the past few months have given much more attention to literature than ever before.

In book distribution we have seen here a striking example of what American methods will do.   Late in the 'nineties two American business men came over to London from Chicago.   They thought that the plan of selling books by instalment had not been properly worked in this country.   At that time the *Encyclopaedia Britannica* was regarded as an absolutely dead book; it could be obtained from any ordinary bookseller's at about half its nominal price, and it is doubtful if a couple of dozen copies were sold in a year.   These strangers bought certain publishing rights in the *Britannica*, and went round to newspaper after newspaper asking their co-operation in selling the book. Newspaper managers laughed at them, and with one accord declared the scheme impracticable, if not an insane one.   At last, almost hopeless, they approached the *Times*.   The *Times* took up their ideas.   There is no one in England but knows the results.   By skilful advertising by " booming " on a system which amounted almost to genius, these Americans sold the once dead book by the score of thousand.   They have since taken up expensive work after expensive work on the same plan, and newspaper publishers who once turned from them now eagerly bid for their favour.   The lowest estimate of the profit earned by these two Americans is a quarter of a million sterling.   The most knowing people in the publishing trade place their gains very much higher.

American " instalment " firms have actually created a new subsidiary calling, that of the " jollyer." The " jollyer " is a smart collector of overdue accounts. If a man falls behind in his instalments he is very rarely or never sued. The "jollyer," who has several shorthand writers and typists helping him, devises innumerable plans to extract the money. In nine cases out of ten he will succeed, even if the backward payer is covered four deep by writs and summonses. He cajoles, he bullies if necessary, he brings pressure on the defaulter's friends, but he gets his money. Jollying, so far, has mainly been carried out in America, and seems to have its centre in Chicago. But there is likely soon to be a field for it in London.

This year Americans are coming into a new section of the British book world, where they promise to repeat their success in other departments. The " Book Lovers' Library " was begun in Philadelphia early in 1900, and in a few months spread throughout the United States. It had no serious competition, there having been no general lending library in America up to the time of the inception. Its founder was Mr. Seymour Eaton, a young Canadian. Mr. Eaton and his colleagues intend covering this country with one operation. Their first idea was to have regular deliveries, largely by their own vans, in every part of England and Scotland. One of their great methods is to deliver books to their clients in all parts for one fixed subscription. They issue their books in card-board cases, and take great care to keep them clean. But they do much more than merely lend books. The Library draws up schemes of reading, issues special catalogues, and is in a large measure an educational as well as a book-distributing agency. It has formed, for instance, a "Book Lovers' Reading Club," with reading courses prepared in many cases by some of the most eminent authorities in Europe and America. This naturally lends itself to the American more than it would to the English mind.

One of the strikingly novel methods which the "Book Lovers' Library" is now pushing in America, and will probably introduce into this country, is the Penny in the Slot Book Circulating Library. The Tabard Inn Library, as this new section of the venture is called, reduced the circulating library principle to the simplest form. Cases containing new books, the selection being constantly changed and the books of the best and in the best of bind-ings, are placed in chemists' shops and in stores in all parts of America. Persons send 12s. 6d. for their opening subscription, and then pay five cents ($2\frac{1}{2}d$.) for each time they change a book, the only formality necessary being to bring the old book back to the library case, give in a five-cent ticket, and take out a new book.

The great English libraries are, I understand, already waking up to the danger of this new com-petitor. They will do well to do so, for the "Book Lovers' Library" and the men behind it are not to be despised. When in Philadelphia, in the autumn of 1901, I went over their headquarters and was much impressed by the business-like management of the whole affair. There was a smartness and a brightness about the way of doing things, and (one can only use the Americanism) a " snap " that did much to explain the phenomenal success the Library had already secured in America. Mr. Eaton was very frank about his hopes here. One thing he has found a great success in America, and which he then hoped also to maintain in England, is the limitation of membership for the ordinary library. In place of, as in the old style, practically any person being able to go to it, pay his subscription and take out books, each would-be subscriber must first be approved by the Library committee. This is no mere formality. Before the approval is made the authorities discover the real facts about the subscriber's home and calling. Those living in unhealthy or dirty surroundings, those socially objectionable, and those in any way in contact with disease are entirely excluded. But at the time of writing this it seems probable that the new venture will adopt more the " slot " system in its raid on this country.

" Only a few days since," said Mr. Eaton to me, " a well-known Episcopal clergyman in New York City proposed three names for membership, and wanted to send the membership subscription to them as gifts, by paying the amount. We were obliged to refuse two. They were hospital nurses, and although they were not dealing with infectious cases, we felt it necessary for the sake of our library as a whole to bar out, however reluctantly, those in constant contact with illness. We are going to be beyond suspicion.

"Another rule we have is that we do not take people of colour. We make this condition on account of the feeling of our members. For instance, if in Washington our book delivery wagons were seen going to the houses of the coloured people every white member there would leave us. Now from a business point of view alone this would not pay us. The consequence of these restrictions is not to injure, but greatly to increase, our growth. You know the old saying that things most difficult to have are most prized. People hearing that they cannot join us at once become anxious to join.

"We expect to get to England in the spring of 1902, and to complete our arrangements during the summer, so as to be able to start operations probably in the autumn."

Mr. Lord, of the Lothrop Publishing Company of Boston, one of the most successful and prudent of the newer houses, tells me :—" The foundations of the new American boom have been advertising and the use of department stores as distributing agents. It has not been by under-selling. The books are usually put at a dollar and a half each (6s. 4d.), published price, and the average price asked by the biggest dry-goods stores is ninety-eight cents (4s. 1d.). The prices paid by the wholesale buyers vary, but may be put at about

3s. 2d., or much the same as the wholesale price of a 6s. book in England.

"The boom has been almost wholly in two things—high-priced works of art and a few novels. A small number of stories sell very largely indeed. But the average tale sells no better now, if so well as it did some time ago.

"You can never tell which book will 'catch on' and which will not. It is largely a matter of caprice. But most of the successful stories have been along these lines. They have dealt with life of a kind about which the reader knew something. The popular tales have been nearly all American stories or stories of English life. Continental fiction stands very little chance. You take a quaint character, such as is to be found in many country parts; you build around him all the anecdotes you know relating to his kind of life, and there you have your story. These popular tales may not be very complex, but they are wholesome, bright, and in some cases largely autobiographical. Clean realism is their note. The authors have learned the secret of looking around them, and using the kind of people they see. Ten years ago the manuscripts submitted to American publishers were mostly 'mushy' and of little value. Now, though every one seems to have taken to writing recently, the average of merit is much higher in every way.

"We advertise. The whole country is placarded about new books, and the posters are made as artistic and attractive as possible. The Saturday literary supplement of the daily papers is used for

advertising purposes, although some of us think
that better advantages are got by advertising in
the ordinary parts of the newspaper than in special
literary supplements.   But you never spend £1,000
for the publishing of a book until you see that that
book has already caught the public taste.

"The department stores now form the great
distributing centres.   These stores buy up very
large quantities of one book at once.   They arrange it in piles, so that every one who enters the
door must see it, and one place alone will perhaps
get rid of a thousand copies in a short time.   The
net result of it all is that the circle of readers of
books has been multiplied fivefold.   People who
never read books before to any extent are now
regular buyers.   The authors are benefited, for
ninety out of every hundred of the books are published on royalty, and the royalties are steadily
rising.   The firm which first introduced this American publishing method into the English book world
will have a fortune.   But none of the older firms
can do it on account of the attitude of their Publishers' and Booksellers' Associations."

Mr. J. E. Hodder Williams, of Messrs. Hodder
and Stoughton and assistant editor of the *Bookman*,
returned from a business visit to America, greatly
impressed by the new methods of bookselling
employed there.   "Where the English publisher
spends a hundred pounds in advertising a single
book—and he does not often do that," Mr. Hodder
Williams declared, "the American publisher spends
thousands.   Not content with merely taking whole

pages in the newspapers for one single novel, he placards the street cars, and you see his posters on the hoardings.

" There are several distinct reasons for the recent record sales of fiction in America. The public immediately reached is larger. I was amazed to see orders for over a thousand copies of a new novel from one central store in such a city as St. Louis, for instance. Then the opening of book departments in the large dry-goods stores, while it has meant practically the abolition of the bona fide bookseller of the old days, has enormously increased the numbers of book readers. These stores buy the one book of the hour in great quantities, and make it a feature of the day's sale, along with the latest lady's ' shirt-waist.' On the day of the publication of Mr. Winston Churchill's new novel, *The Crisis*, there must have been a pile of at least five hundred copies in Wanamaker's big store in New York.

" But this book of the hour sale has its great disadvantages. The novel of the second-class writer, however considerable the merit, has little or no chance.

" Although the American publisher has of course made a fortune out of his great successes, he sees many difficulties looming ahead. Competition between the publishers is forcing up the authors' royalties from the old-fashioned ten to twenty-five, and in at least one case thirty per cent., and the sums paid on account are exceedingly high.

" I do not suggest that all the books which have

reached these tremendous figures were unworthy of their sale. Indeed, some of them, racy of the soil, and making an appeal to the new literary patriotism, deserve their success. But in at least one case a most successful novel was written deliberately according to a recipe supplied by the publisher, who gave the author definite instructions as to the period, the plot, and the characters, and had the manuscript considerably doctored to suit the taste of the public before he issued it. The book was simply rammed down the throats of the American public. But that kind of thing cannot be repeated often. As a matter of fact it would pay a young author to give his first story to one of the booming publishers on any terms, or even to pay the publisher many hundred pounds to force his work to the front, for the advertisement is so great. And once a man has made a hit of this kind his terms rise enormously, and he asks and obtains a higher royalty. In America to-day, to be a young and unknown author is rather an advantage than otherwise, for the great public is constantly waiting for some new idol to acclaim."

One active publisher put it thus to me. " Is the door shut ? " he asked in low tones. " You are sure no one is listening ? I wouldn't have it said under my name for all the world, but the truth is, the old-time publisher has to go. The department stores, like the Whiteley's, the Harrod's and the like, are going to save those of us who throw ourselves into their arms, but they will ruin a good many others first."

N

CHAPTER XVI

THE PRINTING WORLD

THE publishing, bookselling, and newspaper world is in many ways the most conservative section of English industry. Hence the conquest of the literary world by the American is most significant; and undoubtedly on the mechanial side here the American has conquered. In printing machinery the invaders have now almost wholly their own way. In paper they shook our great British manufacturers to the bottom; in ink they are more than successful competitors. In book production they were some years since our humble followers. Now we are becoming their disciples. The American publisher in London is becoming a serious factor, and American book distributing methods are being discussed in every office from Paternoster Row to Albemarle Street.

The progress of the invasion of the paper trade is worthy of note. Five years ago the principal American manufacturers came over here to rush things; they had large surplus products which they were determined to sell at any cost. Ordinary news printing paper was brought down from $1\frac{3}{4}d$. a lb., less ten per cent , to $1d$. a lb. net. The American manufacturers were greatly aided by the very light freight rates across the Atlantic, which cripple those who deliver paper in London, as the cost of carriage from Maine to London is no more than from Cardiff to London. Had the paper makers been at all shaky they must have gone under, when the American would have permanently annexed the trade ; but happily they are, as a whole, firms of very solid financial standing. They stood the full brunt of the fight ; they cut prices to meet the American cuts, and at the same time they put in the newest American machines to lessen their cost of production. Then came the Spanish-American War, which for the time saved the situation, for the demand of news paper was so increased that prices went up again. The Americans have certainly acquired a great deal of the English paper trade, but not so much as was once expected. According to the reports of an English deputation sent last autumn to America, the trade there is now laying down works on such a scale that in a few months we will find ourselves hopelessly underbid. But our paper manufacturers are not yet at the end of their resources.

Turn to printing. Here the American makers are absolutely masters of the field. No first-class daily or weekly paper now when laying down entirely new plant would think of anything but American presses. The main firm in the invasion here has been Messrs. Hoe & Co., of New York, who have

set up large works in England.   It is a commonplace
in the newspaper world that when any journal
wants to improve its plant its ambition is to get
Hoe machines.   They are dear, you have often to
wait some time for delivery, but they are so much
ahead of the older English makes that proprietors
are forced to have them.   But Hoe & Co. no longer
monopolize the making of American machines here.
Recently quite a number of American printing
firms have come over, most of whom import the
parts of their presses.   I may be told, of course,
that Hoe's are now practically an English firm,
since they have their works here.   If this is what
people call an English firm I cannot agree with them.
A house which is directed from New York, which
works from American patterns, of which the cream
of the profits goes to American proprietors, where
the brains, the invention, the skill which make the
thing what it is are all American, can hardly be
spoken of as British, even though it does employ
a certain amount of English labour.

When I once ventured to state that the American
printing presses have all their own way in this
country, I received some very angry denunciations
from English manufacturers, who bluntly told me
that I either did not know what I was talking about
or else had been bribed to boom American goods.
The best answer to them is found in the simple
statement of the machines now in use in the leading
daily newspaper offices in this country.   It is impossible to give the name of every office, but so
far as I can gather them here they are :—

LONDON DAILIES

The Times—mostly English, but some Hoe presses.

The Daily Chronicle—Hoe machines.

The Daily Telegraph—Hoe machines.

The Morning Post—Foster & Sons, Preston.

The Daily Mail—Hoe machines.

The Morning Leader and *Star*—Hoe machines.

The Echo—Hoe machines and one supplied by the Northern Press and Engineering Company, South Shields, in 1899-1900.

The Daily News—English machines.

The Globe—The Victory Company of Liverpool.

The Sun writes : " Of course all the principal daily papers are printed by American machinery, manufactured by Messrs. Hoe & Co.   But it is only fair to state that they have been manufactured in England by English workmen during the last six or seven years, the patents only being supplied from America."

The editor of another leading London daily, while asking me not to mention his name, writes : " I have no objection to saying that, with the exception of two Wharfedales, which are English machines, all our machines are supplied by Messrs. Hoe & Co., and are therefore American machinery.   One or two were, however, I believe, made in London. Our type-setting and distributing machines were supplied by the Empire company, and are therefore also American machines."

Another London daily writes : " The first machines used by us were made by the Victory Company of Liverpool. Then Marinonis were ordered, and finally Hoe & Co.'s machines, which appeared to be the only machines capable of turning out 8, 10, 12, 14, and 16 pages, cut and folded complete."

Still another London daily, while asking that its name should not be specified, says : " The printing presses in use in our office were manufactured by Messrs. Hoe & Co. We have no knowledge of any printing machinery outside that used for newspapers, and have always found Messrs. Hoe's, although more expensive than that of other firms, of higher quality and less costly as regards repairs."

So much for London.

THE PROVINCIAL PRESS

Turn now to the provinces. Some of the leading provincial proprietors have favoured me with their experience. Mr. G. Binney Dipple, the manager of *The Manchester Guardian*, writes as follows :—

" I have no objection to say that we have nine three-roll Hoe machines, made by the great firm who have works both in London and in New York. Some of the machines were made in England and some in America. I think the American ones were slightly superior in finish ; and I noticed various little adaptations and improvements which came first on the New York machines, while those made in England at the same time were without them. The whole of our plant has been bought during the last five years.

" On the whole, I think that the improvements in this class of machinery come from America, but lately the English makers have shown great energy in adopting the American improvements ; and this no doubt is due to the fact that many newspapers have bought their machinery on the other side of the water, and so have given the English manufacturers a strong hint to be more progressive.

" I should like to add a warning to English buyers. Speaking only of the various classes of printing machinery and machinery connected with printing, I think there are a certain number of second-rate machines finding a market here on the ground that they are the latest American speciality, when really they are only second-class work in their own country. I do not like to name instances which I have in my mind, but I think I might state generally that there is a certain danger in jumping to the conclusion that the American machinery over here is better than the English. They make cheap machinery in the States as well as in England, and the Yankee business man is quite willing to take advantage of the boom, and sell what is only a second-class machine in the States at a first-class price here. The only safe way to buy American machinery is to go to America and secure the best class of machinery over there. A great many of the best houses are so full of work on their own side of the water that they do not trouble to push their wares abroad, and the man who has not got full work in America is apt to try to dump his inferior stuff on this side.

" You will see from what I have said that I rather approve of buying American machinery occasionally, if this is done judiciously, as there is no other way of making our own manufacturers see the urgency of their case. As I said above, this has had a good effect upon the printing machine manufacturers in this country.

" A movement with which I have a good deal of sympathy, which is very valuable to this country, is the setting up of large works on American lines in this country, employing British labour. Messrs. R. Hoe & Co. were among the first to do this, and a striking instance of the same kind is the enormous works which the Westinghouse electric company are putting up near the ship canal in Manchester. This is really an importation of the best American brains into English industry, and wherever it occurs you will find the rival English manufacturer bestirring himself very rapidly."

The Scotsman

The Scotsman has recently erected one of the finest newspaper offices in existence. It has searched the world for the most up-to-date plant, and hence the special value of its experience. I am indebted to Messrs. J. Ritchie & Co., the proprietors, for the following :—

" The printing machinery which has been laid down here since 1880 is of British manufacture. The printing presses are all by Messrs. Hoe & Co., London. The latest of these presses was in fact built in New York, but should not be counted as an

American machine, as the order was given to the London firm, and it was only a small matter of arrangement owing to pressure in the London works which brought about the building of the machine in New York.

" All the Linotype machines, of which we have twenty-four, were manufactured at the company's works in Manchester. We are in process of transferring to new offices, and an entirely new equipment of machinery will be installed. The printing presses are being erected by Messrs. Hoe & Co., London. The electric motors, however, which will drive them have been built specially for us at the Bullock Electric Manufacturing Company, Cincinnati, U.S.A. We went very carefully into the question of motors for printing presses, and personal inspection induced us to decide that the motors built for this special purpose in the States had no equal on this side for efficiency."

The Leeds Mercury has Hoe machines.

Sheffield Telegraph

Mr. C. D. Leng, of *The Sheffield Daily Telegraph* and allied publications, writes : " We have two machines which were built in New York, and were the first machines running in England with the V folder. They were made by Messrs. Hoe & Co., of New York, and the London branch has added cover-printing and wire-stitching mechanism. We have the first three-reel machine that was constructed from our design after a visit to the Chicago

Exhibition, where a three-reel 'straight-line' press
was at work. To this machine has been added a
fourth reel printing part. We have a three-reel
machine constructed by the Northern Press and
Engineering Co., of South Shields, and a four-reel
direct-driven printing press constructed by the
same firm. We have a two-reel machine, which
is a Victory-Annand-Hoe combination.

" The American manufacturer has been successful
because he has adopted the best ideas of other
makers, and combined them in one machine. The
English makers stuck too long to their old patterns
and methods. They would not adopt an improvement, lest they should be copying a competitor.
The American manufacturer has no such feeling.
He boldly appropriates any improvement and uti-
lizes it. We can buy to-day American printing
machinery, American paper and American ink at
less money and better quality than English. Those
of us who have travelled in America know the reason
why."

Yorkshire Post

Mr. H. J. Palmer, of *The Yorkshire Post*, writes :
" I may say that we obtain most of our printing
machinery from Messrs. Hoe & Co., who, although
their parent establishment is in New York, have for
many years had large manufacturing works in
London, and at these latter works many of the
machines supplied by them to us have been made.

" Newspaper business men, of course, know that
American supremacy in the class of machinery

which they use is no new thing, but has existed ever since the rotary presses were introduced, nearly thirty years ago. I think this ought to be stated, however, since otherwise the general public may receive the impression that it is some sudden development of American enterprise.

" As to the cause of the success of American printing machinery, I should say it is due to their superior inventive faculty in mechanical engineering."

The manager of a leading Midland daily writes: " I have no objections to informing you that our new printing plant, which was laid down late in 1899, is of American construction; the printing presses and the stereotyping plant being made by the Goss Printing Press Co., of Chicago. The machines which the Goss presses substituted were ' Marinonis ' (three), a French machine, but made, I believe, at Messrs. Sauvées' works in London. These were put down in 189-, when our paper was started. In my opinion the cause of the success of American printing machines in England is the fact that the Americans have made a speciality in building printing machinery, and certainly lead the way in swift rotary presses. Any one who has had the privilege of seeing the magnificent machines at work in the New York and Philadelphia newspaper offices cannot but be impressed with the fact that on the mechanical side, at least, of newspaper enterprise, the Americans lead the way."

The Daily Record and *Daily Mail*, Glasgow, have Hoe machines, and Fosters, of Preston.

Defending English Presses

I am glad, however, to be able to give two letters on the other side, for it is certainly no purpose of mine to withhold any word that can be said in favour of English makers.   Mr. A. J. Jeans, of *The Liverpool Daily Post and Echo* sends to me a strong defence of English machinery.   Says he : " Since 1880 I have had ten or twelve new printing machines, not one of which is American.   Before ordering two large double machines, some four or five years ago, I went pretty exhaustively into the question of machinery, and I came to the conclusion that the English makers were quite as good, if not better than American.   This opinion was fortified when I went for a visit to the States last year, and saw more extensively than I had seen in this country the American presses.

" We have now in our establishment four double presses and several single ones, all of which have been made by the Northern Engineering Co., South Shields.   I don't think America could produce stronger or more perfect presses.   Some of the American makers try to tempt newspaper proprietors by asking lower prices, but, when everything is considered, I don't think we would have gained anything, even in price, by bringing machines from the other side of the Atlantic."

Mr. W. Martin, of *The Newcastle Daily Leader*, writes : " The whole of the printing machinery in use in these offices is of English make.   We have had no experience of American machinery, and we are abundantly satisfied with the type of three-roll machine built by the Northern Press and Engineering Co., South Shields."

It would be a mistake to suppose that the fast rotary press is the whole of the American invasion of the printing world. This invasion extends to everything—from flat bed presses for printing the most delicate illustrations down to automatic proof-pullers. The American folding presses get through twice or three times as much work as the English. The American type-setting machines have revolutionized the art of the compositor. And so one might go on through all the minor apparatus which interests none but those in the trade.

CHAPTER XVII

THE COLONIAL MARKETS—CANADA

IF the American trade invasion of our Empire extended only to Great Britain it would be less ominous for our manufacturers. Had the home market alone been taken from us, we could still find prosperity in our old fields abroad. But in every colony America to-day is fighting for British trade, and America fights, except in the case of Canada, on equal terms with the mother-land.

A paragraph from a recent report of the United States Consular Agent at Eibenstock is well worth attention : " The manufacturer of iron and steel has the greatest interest in the British Empire as a market," he wrote. " His exports to England may be proportionately small, but in the colonies he i advancing by strides and bounds. He has more to hope for from these colonies in the future than from other countries. Our bridge builders are busy in India and Egypt. Our steel rails, machinery and galvanic wires are in South Africa. British enterprise and stability in all these countries means increased opportunities and markets for our manufacturers. Cordial relations with Great Britain will carry us many a milestone on the way. We have thousands of labourers and skilled workmen who are dependent for their existence upon the sale of over-productions. England is our best customer for over-production in food stuffs. The British colonies present the greatest field for our manufactured products."

Canada perhaps affords the field which the Briton can survey with least dissatisfaction. Neighbourliness often leads to rivalry, and the closeness of Canada to the United States has led to keen emulation between the two peoples. For long Canada was a feeding ground for the Republic. People were attracted to our Dominion from Europe, often at great expense and after much trouble, only quickly to go across the border-land. The youngest, the most progressive, the most ambitious of Canadians, looked on it almost as a matter of course in many instances, that when they wanted a wider career they should go to the United States. Canada found its industries strangled at birth by the crushing competition of the protected manufactures of America. Even a high tariff wall did little to protect it. Men on both sides who plumed themselves on their foresight, wrote and spoke of the inevitable day when Canada, sucked dry and overwhelmed by her imperious neighbour, must humbly crave admission to the Union.

That prospect has changed. Canada, with great industries now beginning, with trade rapidly growing, is to a certain extent turning the tables. Canadian iron is competing, and competing severely, with American. American farmers are being drawn into Canada. The flow has reversed from southwards to northwards.

Yet this very turning of the tide has supplied the most vivid proof of the reality of the American invasion of Canada. Formerly America let Canada to a certain extent alone. Now American capitalists are coming in with abundant funds at their back, and are taking over and promoting the enterprises which are adding new fame to the Dominion. The Canadian railway system threatens to become a mere accessory to Mr. Pierpont Morgan's group. The Canadian iron mills, which will soon be a most formidable factor in the world's markets, are being directed to a certain extent from the United States.

It is no fault of the Canadian authorities that America, rather than England, is taking the main hand in the great revival there. Sir Wilfred Laurier and the Liberal Government of Canada, inspired by motives of real patriotism, have done all in their power to cultivate trade with England instead of with the United States. To this end they devised the Preferential Tariff, giving goods imported from England a rebate of twenty-five per cent. over those coming from America. This was found insufficient, so the rebate was made still greater. In other words, the English manufacturer is, and has for several years, been given a bounty for all the goods he sends into Canada.

Nor is this all. The Canadian Government, by close personal work in this country, has sought to arouse British traders to the possibilities of the Canadian market. It affords them facilities of every kind. Canada has practically gone hat in hand to England, begging the old land to increase commercial relations with her. The Government has been splendidly backed up by the enterprise of the Canadian people. *The Toronto Globe* has for some time had offices opened in the heart of London, has prepared and circulated admirable artistic literature about Canada, and has boomed the Dominion in many ways. Other Canadian papers have done the same. The Dominion Government office in London has acted the part of a really efficient business centre. Canada has done its share, and more than its share, but the result has been a bitter disappointment.

English traders have received the Canadian approaches with either indifference or sneers. Not long since, as a case in point, it was stated that the Canadian Government would give a liberal bounty for a fast steamship line running direct from England to the Dominion. On this one English journal declared that English traders wanted no bribes; they could do what they wanted without doles. This is typical.

The way in which England has failed to take advantage of the opportunity in Canada may best be seen by an examination of the official figures. Take, as an illustration, the imports into Canada from Great Britain, and from the United States since the starting of the Preferential Tariff. These show which country is holding its own :—

o

IMPORTS TO CANADA

FROM

Great Britain.		United States.	
1898	£6,573,201	1898	£17,380,140
1899	£7,389,093	1899	£20,328,590
1900	£9,094,458	1900	£23,394,510
1901	£8,632,859	1901	£23,861,355

What do these figures mean ?   Simply that with a heavy preference in his favour, a rebate of no less than one-third in the Customs' duties, the Englishman cannot send to Canada in competition with the American.   The closer the Canadian returns are analyzed the greater is the failure of British traders there shown up.

The American acquisition of railways has assumed serious proportions this past few months.   At the end of January Dr. Seward Webb and a group of American capitalists purchased the Canada Atlantic Railway for ten million dollars.   Dr. Webb is vice-President of the Vanderbilt system of railways, and a son-in-law of Mr. Vanderbilt.   The new owners are about to make very great developments in this line.   The railway is to be improved, as are its western steam ship connexions, in order to obtain the greatest possible share of the grain trade, passenger, freight and package business.   A new grain elevator, with a capacity of 2,500,000 bushels, is to be constructed at Depôt Harbour, the present terminus.   New elevators are to be built at Sorel, in Quebec.   A large amount of the grain trade is to be diverted from the United States to Canada, and it is probable that large steamers will be placed on the upper lakes to augment the tourist traffic. At Ottawa a new central station is to be erected, and a thousand box cars and several locomotives added to the equipment, while heavier rails are to be laid down.[1]

Before this the New York Central had secured the Montreal and Sorel or South Shore Railway and the Rutland Railway. They control railways extending from Depôt Harbour, on the Parry Sound, to Levis, opposite Quebec. The Vanderbilts hold one-half of a possible Canadian trans-continental line.

Naturally these developments are welcomed by many Canadians. Men interested in their Dominion must rejoice in seeing such growth, whoever the growth is promoted by. Thus President Ames, of the Board of Trade, speaking on January 29, after the publication of the news that American capitalists had acquired the Canadian Atlantic Railway, said : " It is of course natural that this step should be regretted by those who favour Government ownership, but it is certainly an evidence that the shrewd business men of the United States are recognizing the value of Canadian investments. We might on imperial grounds prefer that British, rather than American capital, should find investment here. But Americans have the great advantage of proximity. They make their investments on their own judgments, so that there is no fear of those charges of bad faith which sometimes follow the floating

[1] While these pages are going through the press news comes that a hitch has occurred which may delay this deal.

of Canadian enterprises in London.   The same
considerations apply to the settlement of farmers
from America.   They know the West, and can
make personal inspection of the land with comparatively little expense of time and money before
pulling up stakes."

The most important part of the American invasion of Canada has been the attempt to acquire
control of the Canadian Pacific Railway.   The
7,000 shareholders of this line are so widely scattered
that it is difficult for any syndicate secretly to
secure sufficient holdings to control the Company.
But much is being done.   Canadian Pacific stock
is being quietly taken up, and at any time the
thunder clap may come.   A few weeks since the
Hon. Mr. Tarte, discussing the matter in the Dominion Parliament, said that in such an event
Parliament would see that action was taken by the
Government to prevent the deal.   A hundred
millions had been expended in money and land on
this line, and, owing to its value and position, it
must remain always as a Canadian line.   But while
parliamentarians are talking these capitalists are
acting.

The invasion by American capitalists has in many
ways greatly benefited Canada.   Thus, the taking
over of the Leyland line led to an immense development of the grain shipping business from Quebec,
the American railway group diverting much traffic
which formerly went by the Eastern States of
America to that city.   Now that the Dominion line
has also been   acquired   by the American group,

still more is likely to be done. Canada will be the great grain route of the future. American capital and American enterprise are arranging transit lines from Buffalo by the St. Lawrence to the open sea. The grain haul from the West to the Atlantic seaboard by way of Canada is bound enormously to increase year after year in the immediate future. This increase will be in American hands. More than this, it is expected that the carriage of structural steel to ship-board will be by the Canadian waterway, owing to the cheapness in rates, and convenience in handling. The diversion of business to Quebec is only as yet in its beginning. America realizes, if England does not, the splendid field Canada presents. The Leyland line, for instance, is now furnishing a service of large modern steamers, each ten days between Quebec and London, and negotiations are in progress for lines to Manchester, Liverpool and other parts.

One interesting incident in the struggle between Canada and the United States has been the successful effort of the Canadian Government to attract immigrants from the Western States to Western Canada. All along the Canadian Pacific route, between Calgary and Edmonton, a stream of people is pouring in. Some time since the Canadian Government organized a scheme by which agencies were opened in every State where immigrants might be expected, with 250 sub-agents, who are paid so much on commission for every immigrant they can induce to come and settle in Canada, three dollars being paid for a man, and two dollars for a woman. Canadian products are exhibited as samples. The cheapest possible rates of travel are provided, and every practical inducement to practical people is given. Even in the matter of allegiance the American taking up a free homestead can remain a citizen of his native land till three years later, when the Government patent or deal is issued. Then he need only take a simple oath of allegiance to the Canadian constitution, and is not required to renounce his homeland. This oath confers political and all other rights. Four times as many Americans came into Canada last year as ever before.

In the industrial life the American invasion has brought about the development of the great iron and mineral resources of the Dominion. It was long impossible to obtain capital for working these. British financiers had been approached for many years, but had as a rule declined to listen. Now the Americans have come in. They are wise enough to see that while the tendency in America is to-day towards free trade, there is coming a certain reaction in England in favour of preferential tariff within the Empire. They are ensuring that if such a tariff ever does come they will have facilities for competing against our own makers with goods manufactured within the Empire. They see, too, that Canada has natural resources which even the United States cannot surpass. Therefore they are building up in Canada an iron and steel industry which threatens soon even more seriously to compete with our English trade than that of the United

States. Both the Provincial and Dominion Governments of Canada are nursing their infant steel industry in the most careful fashion. By liberal bounties, by big orders for many years ahead, they are making the way of the New England capitalists a path of roses. In Nova Scotia, at Cape Breton and elsewhere, American mills are springing up as fast as they can be constructed.

At Sault St. Marie, at the lower end of Lake Superior, one of the most gigantic steel centres of the world is now in course of construction. Already about £2,500,000 has been spent, and plans are passed for immediately investing nearly as much again. The Canadian Government gave to the companies working there 5,500,000 acres of land, a subsidy of a million dollars for rail construction, and contracts for between four and five million dollars' worth of steel rail, to be delivered during the next five years. The work is now going on there on a Titanic scale. At one spot forests are being stripped of their trees, nearly a thousand men clearing twenty-five acres a day. Enormous mills, giant canals, magnificent steamships, harbours and docks, are all springing up as though by magic. A six-hundred ton rail mill will be in working order this year. Americans are at the back of this.

At the meeting of the Dominion Iron and Steel Company Mr. M. Whitney, the President, told his shareholders that the company is now shipping its products all over Canada, as well as to the United States and Great Britain. This company has a capital of £5,600,000. In Nova Scotia the Vander-

bilts are said to be behind a gigantic scheme known
as the Dominion Securities Company, aiming to
control Nova Scotian transport, and to "boss"
that province as Newfoundland has been bossed by
the Reids. But this is only the beginning. None can
carefully study the Canadian Press without learning
that the people there are resolved to have one of
two things—either a preferential tariff within the
Empire, or reciprocity between Canada and the
States. England cannot keep for ever, and probably will not keep long, the position of the specially
favoured nation. There is no reason why she should,
for our traders have not shown themselves worthy
of the privilege. Canada has up to now taken from
us £750,000 worth of iron and steel a year. That
trade is practically over. The arrangements of the
Canadian Government have given it its death blow.
We may soon have to fight for our three and a half
millions of woollens, cottons, etc.; to put it more
plainly, there is many a lassie in Nottingham and
Manchester may go hungry through the American
raid on Our Lady of the Snows.

It is possible that a Joint High Commission will
meet before long to discuss the trade issues between
Canada and the United States. If America then
shows the slightest reasonableness, some form of
reciprocity will be obtained. Mr. J. Charlton, M.P.,
the distinguished Canadian politician, in a speech
before the Detroit Bankers' Association, voiced the
Dominion's demands. "What is the kind of trade
policy Canada wants with the United States?" he
asked. "She wishes a fair-trade policy. She asks

for no favours. She simply desires to receive fair treatment and fair play, and the privilege of selling something in return for her willingness to buy, with the prospect always had in view that she would, under any conceivable condition of affairs, buy more from the United States than she will send to her." This is not a very promising outlook for English trade.

CHAPTER XVIII

THE COLONIAL MARKETS—SOUTH AFRICA AND AUSTRALASIA

" To the distinguished representatives of the commercial interests of the Empire whom I have the pleasure of meeting here to-day, I venture to allude to the impression which seemed generally to prevail among our brethren across the seas—that the Old Country must wake up if she intends to maintain her old position of pre-eminence in Colonial trade against foreign competition."—The PRINCE OF WALES, at the Guildhall, London, December 5, 1901.

IN writing of trade in South Africa we have to deal with the future rather than the past. For over two years all ordinary business has remained still, and to-day, at the beginning of a new era, South Africa stands as the great market of the immediate future. Now that peace has come South Africa wants literally everything, from pulpits to cradles, and from locomotives to pincushions. The whole of the vast territories devastated by the war have to be re-stocked, and the return of the armies of prisoners of war and their resettlement on the land, aided by grants from our Government, presents trading possibilities such as we of this generation have never seen before.

British blood bought these new dominions, British taxpayers paid, and are paying, the hundreds of millions for the war, while to-day the British flag floats from Tanganyika to Cape Town. But the coming months may show that we have paid the price to benefit the traders of other lands, and that Americans especially will reap the commercial profits of our triumph in South Africa.

There are many reasons that give Americans the advantage here. For one thing, American engineers are largely supreme in the mining districts. . Mine owners tell me that the coming of the American mining engineers, headed by Mr. Hays Hammond, a few years ago, meant a transformation of many properties from losing into very profitable concerns. The position which the Americans then gained they have never lost.

Again, the Americans have for some months, in fact since soon after the beginning of the war, been preparing for the coming trade, in a way which our home houses do not appear to have done. Against these two facts stand out. Certain of the British mine owners are doing their best to keep the trade in their own circle for British houses. And shipping facilities favour England, though the handicap for America here is likely to be quickly removed.

On mining equipment alone within the next five or six years about £30,000,000 will be spent. There will probably be a very great extension of light railways in all parts. There is at least a possibility that, apart from the Cape Colony Government, contractors may be obliged to obtain not only their finished products, but also so far as possible their raw material from British sources.   This is now done in Natal, and has always been found to work well.

Already very large orders are being placed in America for South Africa, orders that seem to promise it much of the trade.   The De Beers Company has sent Mr. Gardner Williams to the United States, where he is buying machinery and equipment, including even structural material.   The South African Breweries, Ltd., a company spending £160,000 on a new brewery in Cape Town, is having it designed in America, and everything, except the bricks and mortar, is to be from there.   Another brewery, also being built in Johannesburg, was designed in New York, and all the supplies for it are coming from America.   One New York house has secured the contract for the structural iron and steel work, another for the copper work ; the steel tanks, fermenting and storage tanks come from Pennsylvania ; the cooker from New York ; the refrigerating plant from Buffalo ; while a Chicago firm is supplying the brewing machines and driving device.

These are but signs.   A long list of similar advance orders could be given.   On this point I cannot do better than quote an admirable article in a recent issue of the *British and South African Export Gazette* :—

" The causes of the preponderating share of foreign countries in mining machinery exports are several, some being natural and others accidental, and the knowledge of their character will assist to understand the nature of the obstacles to be overcome by our manufacturers to secure an augmented share of these orders. The first and natural reason, against which little headway can be made, is the large amount of foreign capital which is locked up in the Transvaal gold mines. It is said that Germany and France have as much as £50,000,000 so invested, which factor has, of course, a great influence in controlling the country of origin of the machinery supplies. Another factor, which is of the accidental kind, is the large number of American engineers, etc., who are employed in the South African mining industry, both of gold and diamonds. Wittingly or unwittingly, they are the cause of the divergence of no inconsiderable amount of valuable orders to the land of their birth. Allusion has recently been made to a glaring case of this kind where orders for machinery equipment to the extent of a million and a quarter sterling for the Robinson group of mines—an English capitalized group—were placed in the United States solely from the fact that the disposal of them lay in the hands of the consulting engineers and other American officials of the mine. Other causes for the diversion of business to the foreign firms are the ceaseless energy, adaptiveness, and superior business methods of their representatives in the several mining centres, as well as the fact that they employ a highly technical local staff, and carry large and representative stocks in their branch warehouses on the several fields. These latter factors are of the nature of accidental aids, and are remediable in proportion as British firms show equal or superior enterprise and initiative."

The Cape Government has shown itself especially favourable to American firms. This, the Cape Government officials declare, is because they cannot obtain the goods they require, more especially railway material, in the time or at the prices they need. They give British contractors a preference of ten per cent. ; further than that they refuse to go. The result has been that large orders for the Cape Government railways have been supplied by America, and more will be in the immediate future. In one year America's exports to South Africa have risen from £4,127,428 to £6,095,636. And this is only the beginning.

Australia is still mainly in British hands for trade, and the people have a strong prepossession in favour of British goods. But the Americans are making special efforts to conquer the Commonwealth, and not wholly in vain. They are greatly aided by the work of the " Conference " of shipping brokers in London, which keeps up the freight rates between England and Australia. The President of the Melbourne Chamber of Commerce, speaking on this matter in September last, said : " With three great countries regular lines of steamers have been established, and the rates of freight paid are without exception lower than those from Great Britain. So severe was the competition in freights from the United States to Australia some time ago that 8s. 6d. and 10s. per ton, C.F., was accepted, compared with 47s. 6d. and 60s. from ports in Great Britain ; and even now, although the lines of English-owned steamers trade regularly with Australia from New York, their freights are as a rule half those from English ports, being 20s. to 30s. per ton from New York and 40s. to 70s. from Great Britain. . . . Their power (that of the Conference) is a serious menace to the trade of the Empire, for, securing as they do all the British trade at high rates, they arrange for the exclusion of competition with the foreign lines, and in consequence drive a large portion of our legitimate trade into foreign countries."

The low freights existing between the Pacific Coast and the Australasian Colonies have greatly aided American commerce. Perhaps the most marked results have been in the colony of New Zealand, where in three years the American imports have risen from £628,044 to £1,061,873. American trade with Australia began with sailing vessels bringing over kerosine oil. Then came the start of a regular service of steamers from San Francisco to Sydney. In 1881 exports and imports combined amounted only to about two millions a year ; to-day they reach seven and a half millions, and are going up by leaps and bounds. The boot trade has largely been taken out of English hands ; the Tobacco Trust is seeking to annex the land. The American invasion of Australia has barely begun. One of the most popular of Agents-General, writing to me, says : " Americans are handicapped by the absence of an adequate merchant marine. When they have one the conditions will undergo a great change. There

will be an ' invasion ' then, without any fear of mis-
construction of the term. Now if locomotives, to
mention only one article, are ordered, they are
almost certain to be had from England, for otherwise
constant supervision is necessary. The Baldwin
firm are, however, able to undertake delivery from
America to Australia, and do occasionally get orders.
When all American firms can do this, the difference
will be immediately and appreciably felt in England.
Nor will it be long before this is the case. Tramps as
big as the *Oceanic* are being built expressly for the
mercantile marine, and the old conditions are on
the eve of change. America's energies are being
directed to this end.

" The most important event in the history of trade
between America and Australia was the International Conference, held at Philadelphia in 1899.
Its object was avowedly the capture of the world's
trade for America, and its effect was immediate, as
may be seen from statistics. A similar Conference
is urgently needed in England. The whole case has
been placed before Mr. Chamberlain, but up to now
nothing has come of it."

CHAPTER XIX

SPORT

THE future historian will probably record that the greatest promoter of the Anglo-American alliance was not commerce, not even the ties of blood or language, but athletics. The Englishman may yield tribute to the one who surpasses him in commerce, but he gives ungrudging respect to the rival who can stand up against him in sport. This the American has done.

Both in Britain and the United States the picked gladiators of either nation have met for half a century, and the athletic competitions between the two nations grow more numerous as the years pass on. In America amateur sport is a much more serious business for the men who take it up than with us. They train more thoroughly, practically sacrificing everything else for the time to their severe regimen. In England, apart from professional players, sport as practised in our public schools and universities is only one side of a multifold life. In America the 'varsity man who takes up sport has to give himself almost wholly to it.

P

In the years 1900 and 1901 Americans reached the climax of success in British sport. An American owner, Mr. W. Whitney, won the Derby. In University athletics Yale and Harvard left Oxford and Cambridge far behind. In amateur contests the triumph of American competitors was so marked that it was seriously proposed to exclude foreign competitors from one great race. A greater exhibition of weakness than such a proposal has rarely been seen in British athletic circles.

On the turf American jockeys have in recent years revolutionized our riding, and scored win after win. J. F. (Tod) Sloan, Lester Reiff, and John Reiff are the three who led the American invasion here. Sloan made his appearance upon an English racecourse in October, 1897, and by November 6 he had ridden six firsts and three seconds out of a total of twelve mounts—a really remarkable record. During the following season he maintained his position, and so frequently won that he was dubbed " the working man's friend." Success did not suit him, however, and after a deplorable affair at Ascot, in which a waiter was concerned, he ended his career, and the English turf knew him no more.

Sloan introduced the American seat, in which the rider is perched upon the horse's neck, thus getting rid of wind pressure. His example has since been followed to a more or less extent by the majority of English jockeys, Mornington Cannon being a striking exception. Sloan's method of riding was very severely criticized. He was upon the back of the French "Holocauste" when the latter broke a fet-

lock in the Derby, and on the occasion good judges
held that the position of the rider contributed to
the serious nature of the accident, after the horse
had stepped on a bottle thrown carelessly upon the
course by one of the crowd. The success of Sloan
brought many others from America, of whom Lester
and J. F. Reiff secured most public confidence,
although J. H. Martin, D. Maher, and Clem Jenkins
all had their own following.

The great battle for supremacy between English
and American jockeys and trainers was fought in
1900. Sam Loates, the English leader, after holding
a comfortable leading up to the late season, was
eventually beaten by Lester Reiff, the figures of the
latter being :—

L. Reiff (America), mounts 553, wins 143.
S. Loates (England), mounts 810, wins 137.
J. Reiff (America), mounts 604, wins 124.
O. Madden (England), mounts 661, wins 96.
F. Rickaby (England), mounts 476, wins 84.
J. F. Sloan (America), mounts 311, wins 82.
K. Cannon (England), mounts 600, wins 75.
M. Cannon (England), mounts 490, wins 82.
B. Rigby (America), mounts 447, wins 68.
J. H. Martin (America), mounts 327, wins 52.

American horses and jockeys managed to secure
a considerable share of the prizes in 1901, although
Sir J. B. Maple of England headed the list of winning
owners with £20,894, Mr. W. C. Whitney of America
being second with £19,820 10s. So far as the jockeys
were concerned Otto Madden (English) held the lead
almost from the start for flat racing, but Tod Sloan

and S. Loates were running a neck and neck race for the second place for a long while. The former lost his licence early in October, and Loates ran into a pedestrian and fractured his thigh in the autumn, thus destroying his chance of figuring near the top of the list. The figures of the latter at the finish were :—

O. Madden (England), mounts 676, wins 130:
D. Maher (America), mounts 420, wins 94.
G. McCall (England), mounts 451, wins 91:
J. Reiff (America), mounts 482, wins 89.
S. Loates (England), mounts 522, wins 84.
L. Reiff (America), mounts 322, wins 75.
M. Cannon (England), mounts 450, wins 76.

At Henley Regatta—Royal Henley, as it is generally termed—the American invasion has become very real, so real indeed that at the end of 1901 the stewards were asked to deal with the question of foreign entries. A strong section demanded that such rules should be framed as would bar out Americans. The feeling of the clubs, however, was that amateur entries would be received, nineteen voting in favour of this to five against. So matters will go on as before.

In 1894 J. Ryan, the well-known Toronto sculler, was one of the entrants at Henley, but he was knocked out in the heat in the Diamond by our Guy Nickalls. In the following year (1895) Cornell University entered for the Grand, and in the third heat a misunderstanding occurred with Leander. But as the visitors did not succeed in wresting the premier honours from our lads, nothing was lost beyond the ink that was spent over the occurrence, although Cornell were acting strictly within the letter of the law in pursuing the course they did.

A year later (1896) Yale entered for the Grand at Henley, but it was discovered that its men could only last for about three quarters of a mile, and they were beaten by Leander. In 1897 Teneyok's entry for the Diamond was accepted, and he won the event, although later on it was decreed that he was a professional, and that his name could not be accepted again as a competitor. In winning the Diamond he defeated Blackstaff in the final in record time for the course, although it is only fair to the latter to state he had previously beaten McDonnel, another American, in even faster time. Winnipeg also entered for the Henley of 1897, but was knocked out by New College.

At the Henley of 1899 the Canadians were beaten, but in 1901, which was far and away the most exciting ever known in the history of aquatics, the Americans took many honours. Pennsylvania entered for the Grand, and had done so well in previous contests that the victory of its men was anticipated by the majority of those on the spot. Leander, however, rose to the occasion, and won by a length in seven minutes and five seconds, after a grand race. Leander were led for the greater part of the journey, but towards the end their longer strokes told, and amidst enthusiasm which even Henley has rarely equalled, they first got on terms and eventually got ahead of the Americans. Recognizing the task they had on hand, two of the winning crew on the previous evening scratched for one of the events they had entered.   The method of training pursued by the visitors caused much discussion over accepting entries outside the United Kingdom. After Henley, Pennsylvania crossed to Ireland, and walked away from Trinity College, Dublin, upon the Lake of Killarney.   The proposal to exclude foreign entries was made by Mr. W. H. Grenfell, M.P.

In cycling the name of one American wheelman, A. A. Zimmerman, stands out pre-eminent.   Coming to this country in 1893 he carried everything before him as far as scratch events were concerned.   His riding was a revelation to our men, his final sprint for the tape being something to wonder at.   But his career as an amateur was cut short by the National Cyclists' Union, who declared him to be a professional.   After that he did very little, and is now simply known by reputation.   Another American flier, J. S. Johnston, possessor of many American records, also formed one of the select band brought together to exploit the Simpson lever chain (now dead to the world) at Catford in 1896.   On this occasion Johnston did an exciting ride-flying mile, but failed to equal his figures set up on the other side of the Atlantic.

In amateur athletics America has played a prominent part, her representatives having fairly beaten the whole country in short distance events. In 1894 Oxford University met Yale at Queen's Club, West Kensington, this being the first occasion the two Universities were pitted against one another. The visitors were the favourites, but the Oxonians

secured an unexpected victory, winning five events
to three, a dead heat being registered in the long
jump. In 1897, at the Amateur Athletic Association Championship held at Fallow-field, W. S.
Hipple and R. Sheldon represented America, the
former being successful in putting the weight, beating at the same time the best previous championship performances.

In 1899 came the great competition between Oxford and Cambridge and Yale and Harvard, at the
Queen's Club, West Kensington, when Bowell
(Harvard) won the hammer; Quintin (Harvard)
the 100 yards; Fox (Harvard) the 120 yards hurdle;
and Rice (Harvard) the high jump, the English on
this occasion winning the odd event, the victory of
Davison in the quarter mile turning the tide in the
favour of our men, but losing the 100 yards and the
hurdle, considered to be certainties for them.

In 1900 the Amateur Athletic Championships were
held at Stamford Bridge, and some two dozen
Americans entered. A. F. Duffy (Georgetown) won
the 100 yards in ten seconds; M. W. Long (New
York Athletic Club) the quarter-mile in forty-nine
and four-fifths seconds; J. K. Baxter (Pennsylvania) the high jumps, 6ft. 2in.; A. C. Kraenzlein
(Pennsylvania University) the long jump, 22ft.
10¼in.; B. Johnson (New York A.C.) the pole jump,
11ft. 4in.; J. J. Flanagan (New York A.C.) throwing
the hammer, 163ft. 1in.; R. Sheldon (New York
A.C.) putting the weight, 45ft. 10½in.; A. C. Kraenzlein the hurdles, in fifteen and two-fifths seconds,
the latter being the world's record for grass.

The season of 1901 was scarcely of such an interesting character, although a few of the Americans were present at the Amateur Athletic Championships at Huddersfield. A. F. Duffy retained the hundred yards; A. E. Kraenzlein retained the hurdles; J. K. Baxter tied in the pole runs and won the high jump. A team from Oxford and Cambridge also visited the United States, and met Harvard and Yale at Berkeley Oval, near New York, being beaten by six events to three.

Professional running has lacked interest of late years. E. C. Breden, formerly a member of the London Athletic Club, beat C. K. Kilpatrick, reputed to be one of America's star performers, in 1897, at 600 and 800 yards, a third match, 1,000 yards, being rendered unnecessary. The lessons of the amateur meetings are that in short-distance events the Americans are our superiors, but they lack the stamina necessary for an extended effort.

There are some branches of sport in which Americans cannot touch us. Thus in football and cricket we hold undisputed sway. In billiards again we have J. Roberts, the world's premier player, H. W. Stevenson, a professional, and Charles Dawson, the ex-champion, this trio being far in advance of any cueist who has visited these shores from the other side of the Atlantic. No attention need be paid to the match in which Ives and Roberts took part, in which the former made a break of 2,540, for the table had been altered, or the position could never have been secured. The balls were two and three-quarter inches in diameter, and the pockets three and a quarter inches wide. Ives, four nights from the commencement of the match, got the balls into one of the corners, jammed them there, thus forming what is termed an " anchor," and he might have played on for a year and a day had he felt so inclined. He made 2,540, and thus broke up the position purposely, but getting it again on Saturday, the last day, ran out with a lead of 892. This was not, however, English billiard playing, and the ball could not be jammed on a table built in accordance with rules of the Billiard Association of Great Britain. In tricks and in fancy strokes our leading professionals have undoubtedly something to learn from their American cousins, but in billiards as played in ordinary matches they are unapproachable.

In yachting we frankly take off our hats to our Transatlantic rivals. Have they not got and kept the Cup in spite of our best endeavours ?

Since the days when the American Cup was taken across the Atlantic by an American boat there have been persistent attempts on the part of the yachtsmen of Great and Greater Britain to bring the coveted trophy back again. England, Scotland, Ireland and the Canadian Dominion have all entered into the struggle.

It was in 1851, on the occasion of the World's Fair, that the reputation of the New York boats for swiftness caused the suggestion that as there would be an unusual collection of yachts at Cowes that year the New York Yacht Club should send a representative yacht to sail in an international match.

As the result of this the schooner *America* was sent over. It found some difficulty at first in securing races, and afterwards a challenge was made to sail first against any schooner, and then any schooner or cutter. This producing no result, a challenge was made to sail the *America* in a match against any British vessel for any sum from one to ten thousand guineas, the only stipulation made being that the breeze should be at least six knots an hour. This challenge was not accepted. In disgust, the Americans said they would take their vessel back at once. It was then pointed out to them they might sail here in the Cowes Regatta on August 22 of that year. There was no time allowance, and no limit, and the course was from Cowes round the whole of Wight. The prize was a Cup presented by the Royal Yacht Squadron. The race lasted from 10 a.m. to 8.35 p.m., the *America*, as all the world knows, coming in as winner, and thus taking the Cup across the Atlantic. British builders were annoyed at the success. They declared they could easily build a boat in ninety days to beat the *America*. They offered a prize of £500 for another race, but the Americans declined to stay for such a period unless the prize were raised to £5,000. This was refused, and the *America* sailed back. The Cup was presented to the New York Yacht Club as a perpetual challenge Cup.

For many years it remained in undisputed possession of its owners, but a second race was arranged in 1870. Mr. James Ashbury, an Englishman, after a series of challenges, took across the famous yacht called the *Cambria*. She had to sail against an American fleet, and was thoroughtly beaten by an American boat called the *Magic*. Next year the same Englishman built a boat called the *Livonia*. Two American yachts, the *Columbia* and the *Sappho*, proved too much for her, and after spending £22,000 Mr. Ashbury had to give up his designs on the American Cup.

In 1876 the Canadians came on the scene. Mr. Charles Gifford, Commodore of the Canadian Yacht Club, entered a yacht called the *Countess of Dufferin*, but an American yacht called the *Madeleine* proved a swifter sailer in two races.

There was no further contest till 1881, and then it was in response to a Canadian challenge. The Bay of Quinte Yacht Club sent the *Atalanta* under Captain Cuthbert, but she met with no greater success than the *Countess of Dufferin*. The American yacht was named the *Mischief*.

Four years elapsed, during which came the rise of the cutters, and in 1885 one of the most popular challengers who have ever crossed the ocean took across one of the most dangerous competitors. The challenger was Sir Richard Sutton, and his boat was the *Genesta*. A young American designer was called in to plan something in an emergency, and he combined the best points of the English and the American designs. It was known as a compromise model, and is really the foundation of modern yachting boats. His name was Edward Burgess, and his boat was called the *Puritan*. She defeated the dangerous *Genesta*.

A year later Lieutenant Henn with his *Galatea* unsuccessfully tried to lift the Cup, defended by *Mayflower*. 1887 saw Scotland making a determined bid for the Cup. Vice-Commodore Bell, of the Royal Clyde Yacht Club, took over the famous boat the *Thistle*. She sailed two races with the *Volunteer*, a boat belonging to General Paine, also designed by Burgess. The result did not affect the domicile of the Cup.

The Earl of Dunraven was the next to appear on the scene. He built the first of the *Valkyries*, but no race came off owing to some absurd squabble about the conditions, in which Lord Dunraven was not to blame. But in 1893 with another *Valkyrie* he crossed the Atlantic. Four American yachts were built, and the best of these, the *Vigilant*, was chosen to defend the Cup. After two magnificent races the *Valkyrie* was defeated. Undeterred, the Earl of Dunraven in 1894 took across *Valkyrie III*. This was the most exciting of contests. It was also very unfortunate in its results, as there was considerable ill-feeling created. The *Defender* was the American yacht, and it will be remembered that she won the first race. In the second race there was a foul, which was given against the *Valkyrie* that had won the race. The Earl of Dunraven was so disappointed and annoyed that on the third race he simply brought *Valkyrie* to the line of start and then withdrew her from the race, leaving *Defender* to sail over the course alone and to be declared victor of the series. For five years there was no race. Then came the era of Sir Thomas Lipton, who shares with

Sir Richard Stone the distinction of popularity and esteem.   His two gallant attempts to lift the Cup with *Shamrock* and *Shamrock II.* are too recent to need comment.   Sufficient to say the Cup still remains on that side of the Atlantic where it went in 1851.

CHAPTER XX

THE SECRET OF AMERICAN SUCCESS

AMERICANS are succeeding to-day largely because of their climate, their superior education, their longer working hours, their willingness to receive new ideas, their better plant, and perhaps most of all, because of their freedom from hampering traditions.

It may be noticed that I do not say Americans are succeeding because of the great resources of their country. This I am aware is the common explanation. But although the natural resources of America are one of the great ultimate factors in the contest, it is yet possible to attribute too much importance to them at the present stage. England has magnificent resources, and is placed in a spot which naturally makes her a great centre of the world. Here we have iron, and coal, shipping facilities, and mineral wealth of every kind, and it is not for us to complain of the natural resources of our competitors.

What we must complain about is our bad legislation, our neglected education, our indifference, and excessive optimism. Through our bad legislation we have lost and are losing many trades. The tobacco, printing, and electric industries are instances of this. Once Ireland had flourishing tobacco plantations. These were purposely killed in order that the tobacco industry in our then American colonies might be fostered. Our erstwhile colonies are now a rival nation, but the revenue restrictions still make tobacco growing here practically impossible.

There is no reason, climatic or other, why Ireland to-day should not produce great tobacco crops. A short Act of Parliament fostering the home growth of tobacco by a simplification of the collection of duty, and a rebate—or even temporary remission—of taxes on tobacco grown within the kingdom, would create a new industry in Ireland at a bound. Some of us would, as a matter of taste, prefer the leaf of the nicotina grown in Kilkenny to Schleswig-Holstein cabbages doctored and browned in Hamburg.

In printing we have an immediate example of how legislation affects trade. When in 1893 the United States granted limited copyright to foreign authors it was provided that books, to secure this copyright, must be printed from types set up in the United States, or from plates made from the same; and that the plates and transfers for pictures must be made in America. This law has resulted in transferring the printing of many of our best books to America. Naturally publishers do not care to have the double expense of setting up in both countries, so they import. This practice is increasing every year.

The British compositor suffers. I turn to the current report of the printing trade and find that in district after district business is recorded as "bad," "dull," "poor." At the same time new books by English authors, printed in America, are selling largely here. Cause and effect. And this will grow unless copyright is refused to books not set up in the Empire.

The Americans have a prohibitive tariff on pictorial posters to the extent of twenty cents per pound. This effectually prevents our exporting a single sheet of English printing to their country, while they flood us with their surplus, which they can afford to sell in the English markets at a price which the printers here could not make cover their cost. This they are enabled to do by utilizing their surplus stocks for export without interference with their home prices. As one well-known English firm, Messrs. David Allen & Sons, Ltd., writes: "English printers could not complain of this if they were allowed to do the same, but that is impossible under present tariff conditions. The obvious course under these circumstances is to protect themselves—ere it is too late—by putting a tariff on American printing imported into this country equal to that levied on English printing going into America. Until the principle of retaliation is recognized, the evils we are suffering from by unfair American competition will increase

and multiply. There is no other logical outcome
—let us do as we are done by."

Education is another factor which accounts for
much. The American workman is on the whole
much better educated than his English rival.
Here the idea of elementary education seems to
be to teach as many subjects as possible, and
elementary schools are usually rated according to
the subjects in their time tables. In America,
on the contrary, the aim is rather to increase
intelligence than to give a smattering of multiplied
subjects. Children there are not repressed but
rather encouraged to exercise their intelligence.
The co-education of boys and girls reacts not only
on the moral tone but on the entire intelligence of
the people. There they have a satisfactory system
of secondary education ; between elementary and
secondary education in England a great gulf is
fixed. There the whole of the manufacturing
districts of the north, east, and west are covered
with magnificent technical schools. In England
we simply do not know what technical education
means as carried on in America.

It is easy wholly to blame the British workman
for our retrogression. It is not the workman, but
the limitations under which he labours that are
to blame. American employers declare with one
voice that the English mechanic when he crosses
the Atlantic takes rank with the German as the
finest and most reliable worker.

The conditions under which British workmen
labour are steadily improving. Undoubtedly in

Q

the past he has in this country set his face steadily against labour-saving machinery, and has done his best to limit the output in a thousand ways. Let a new machine be introduced in many callings, and it is the rule for the trade union to fix the maximum amount of work that machine may do. If this is not done openly it is often done in secret. In America a machine is usually worked to the utmost of its capacity. Here it is not.

Some time since a prominent English engineer went over to America and saw there a much improved form of lathe. He ordered it for his own workshops, and put one of his best and smartest men on it. To his surprise the man, after he had had time to became familiar with the machine, only turned out about one-third the work the same apparatus was doing in America. The master put a second on it, but with the same result ; and then a third, but there was no improvement. He taxed the third man with shirking. " You know," he said, " you could turn out three times as much work on that machine if you liked." The man looked stolidly at him. " Yes," he said, " I daresay I could, and I'd get my head split too if I did."

Before the engineers' strike the rule of one man one machine prevailed in British factories. With the modern automatic machine this means simply that the man has nothing to do most of the time. Take, for instance, the automatic screw-turning machine. Here the only work of the man is to put in fresh steel bars, brush the steel shavings on one side, remove the screws, and see that his machine is working properly. In America a man paid perhaps twelve shillings a day manages six or eight of these machines. In England until recently you were allowed to supervise only one. It is true that the worker here received only half the wage. But even this made our labour cost in England from three to four times as much as in America. Since the engineers' strike, things have undoubtedly been much improved. But masters here have not yet got full control of their own workshops.

The same man with the same tools turns out less here than in America. Not only does the western American work longer, but he works harder. In America it takes the work of six or seven men for a year to turn out a locomotive—in England it takes fifteen. Here the mechanic who does too much is a marked man, for other men know that if work is paid by piece, an increase of output will be followed by the reduction of the rate of pay. The United States employers think that the higher wages their men make the better for the masters.

It is easy to understand the reason the British workman desires the little output. He knows that the introduction of labour-saving machinery means a temporary displacement of labour. Now in a country like America, where labour is in good demand and where a man is able to undertake almost everything, this does not so much matter. But in England a man is expected to stick to his trade. If he is a compositor and the linotype throws him on the street, he will not be allowed to start bricklaying or painting to earn his bread. Trade union regulations, customs of the country, and so on, all bar his way. Consequently, the man, though knowing that in the end the linotype may increase the printing business, yet opposes it all he can, well aware that it may mean starvation for his wife and children. We must make labour elastic, if our workmen are to welcome labour-saving machinery.

But after every allowance and consideration is made, the fact remains that limitation of output and the aversion of our workmen to labour-saving machinery, have together operated very heavily against us. In some trades the prejudice has been carried to fatal lengths. Perhaps the most injurious instance, and the one where the Americans have reaped most direct benefit, is in the flint glass trade. The English flint glass maker is one of the most skilled of his craft, and his wares, other things being equal, would capture the world's markets. But the flint glass hands have for generations steadily pursued a policy of stupid short-sightedness. They have limited the number of workmen by forbidding the employment of more than a small proportion of apprentices. They have taken out of the masters' hands altogether the choice of workmen, so that a master must take men the union chooses to nominate when he has a vacancy, rather than those he wishes. They have forbidden the promotion of specially efficient men by making promotion entirely dependent upon seniority. In short they have placed their men at a dead level, and have removed every incentive to special skill or special industry. No man is allowed under any condition to turn out more than a given amount of work, even if his furnace lies idle most of the time. The men have been united and determined, the masters divided, contentious, jealous and eager to reap little advantages over one another. Consequently the masters have delivered themselves wholesale into the men's power, and the flint glass trade, once largely in our hands, has gone in great part to Bohemia, France, and America. American glass of high quality is being sold in this country to-day, not because we cannot produce for ourselves, but because of the obstinate foolishness of our workmen.

Yet in this craft, which admittedly presents one of the worst examples of any, things are improving. In more enlightened trades the workmen's leaders are themselves urging the men to special industry. " Mabon," the famous leader of the South Wales miners, recently publicly admitted that what he had seen in America had converted him to the use of labour-saving appliances, a use which he had formerly opposed. Such a declaration from such a leader is significant of a change coming over our workmen.

It is worth noting that while in England limitation of output is diminishing, there is a tendency in America to begin it. During the past year or two a feeling has been steadily growing among the employees in various manufacturing industries, that they are not going to work too hard. This feeling, so far as one can trace it, is mainly among the foreign immigrants. They prefer more leisure to increased pay. In the labour unions, which are now growing in power, quiet work is going on for limitation of output. How it will end it is too early yet to say.

Mr. Schwab, President of the Steel Trust, puts the limitation of output in England as the bottom reason of our declining prosperity. When giving evidence last year before the United States Industrial Commission he said :

" During a recent visit to England I told the iron and steel manufacturers there that they will never be able to compete with the United States because of the unreasonable rules of the trade unions. In England certain machines are permitted to produce only one-third as much as in the United States, with the result that the cost of production is greatly increased. The difficulty with labour unions to-day is not usually one of wages, but is simply whether the masters will surrender the control of their works to their men."

If our workmen are slow, the masters are often enough right behind the times. In spite of all recent warnings, there is a stolid conservatism about their methods which seems irremovable. Even great houses which have the name of being most progressive, often enough decline to look into new improvements. The American thinks that because a thing is new there is a possibility that it is better than the old. The English master, on the contrary, believes that because a thing is new it is to be treated with the utmost suspicion. In America the workman is encouraged to suggest improvements. In England the workman who did so would, in nine instances out of ten, be snubbed and told to mind his own business. A leading engineer not long since told me that he once secured the rights in a certain locomotive invention of real value. This new method had been tried abroad, and was in use on certain foreign government railways. He communicated with a number of the large users in that line in England. Most of them did not even trouble to reply. One or two wrote curtly refusing to trouble themselves in the matter. Yet here was a method which it had been proved would save them a considerable percentage of their expenditure in one direction. This instance might be multiplied a hundredfold. While our employers as a body are so conservative, they have little right to lecture their workmen.

Two brothers recently visited the offices of a firm of American machine agents in London. One was at the head of an important English manufacturing firm, the second was an engineer who had lived in Pennsylvania for some years. The latter pointed out to his brother machine after machine that he ought to have. "You know, Tom," he at last declared emphatically, "if I were in your place I'd throw every bit of your old machinery on the scrap-heap, and have an up-to-date plant right through. You'd double your output and halve your expenses." Tom listened carefully and put his hand to his chin in reflective fashion. "Well, Dick," he said at length, "you may be right. I won't say that you're not. But why should I change? Th' owd machines were good enough for father, and they were good enough for grandfather, so I am thinking they're good enough for me."

On this point Consul Boyle of Liverpool made some very pertinent remarks to his Government at Washington last December :—

"It is undoubtedly true," said he, "that speaking generally, and quite apart from the question of trades unionism, English manufacturers find it almost impossible to get the same amount of product from machines as is obtained in America. There are two reasons that account for this. . . .

"The first reason is that, as a rule, the British workman is not as adaptable as the American workman—he does not so readily get command of new appliances as the American workman; and the second is that it is not the custom of the country for an Englishman, whether mechanic, clerk, or labourer, to work as hard as an American.

"English trades-unionists who have recently visited the United States as delegates to labour conventions, or in a representative capacity to make observations, as a rule report that American mechanics and factory hands work too hard. An American manager of a match factory established over here with American machinery once told me that 400 people in a factory in America turned out more matches than 700 people over here, with identically the same machinery—and incidentally it may be remarked that practically all the machinery used in the English match factories is American, and has been so for many years. In some respects the English workman is more 'independent' than the American workman—that is, he will not endeavour to make himself so 'handy' and will often refuse to do anything outside a certain line rigidly laid down by the custom of his craft generally and by his trade union in particular. American manufacturers who establish factories here find that, although the English workman is thorough in what he does, he is not only slow in comparison with an American workman, but will sometimes strike on the slightest provocation — although it is observed that within the last two years the leading spirits among trades-unionists have taken a somewhat pronounced position against strikes, except as a last extreme resort. In this connexion it is worth noting that, as a rule, strikes in England are more stubborn than in America, although it is the exception for violence to be used here. Although there is a greater division of labour in America, yet oftentimes twice as many men are required in England to do a certain job as would be required in America, as each man is very jealous lest a workman in another allied trade should do the smallest piece of work which the rules of his trade say should be done by him, and him alone. For instance, when the town hall of Liverpool was recently being remodelled in the interior, there was a strike for several months, owing to the fact that some cabinetmakers did some work which the joiners claimed should be done by themselves alone.   Within the last few days a strike was averted by arbitration at Laird's shipbuilding yard (where the *Alabama* was built), on the Mersey, opposite Liverpool, the dispute being as to whether the engineers or the shipwrights should place an electric dynamo in position.   And there is now a controversy, with threats of a strike, at a port just north of here, between carpenters and ship-wrights, as to who, under trades-union rules, had the right to construct a pier.

"A few weeks ago, some painters who were re-decorating the interior of a church in a midland town ceased work because women were employed to clean the droppings of paint on the pews, and the employers had to finish the job themselves. And quite recently in a seaside town there was a strike of teamsters because their employer re-fused to discharge a driver who had made a journey to a neighbouring town three hours quicker than they themselves had been accustomed to take. A Liverpool architect once told me that he had two large buildings on which there had not been a stroke of work done for over three months, for the reason that a strike had been declared because a plumber's apprentice had been caught by the union ' delegate ' making a joint which the union rules stated should be done by a journeyman. I was informed by the architect that within the last ten years the cost of construction had increased 15 per cent.—owing partly to increase of wages, but principally to the limitations as to a day's work. A cut-glass manufacturer residing in Liverpool tells me that notwithstanding increased mechanical facilities, the output per man has decreased fully 25 per cent. during the last dozen years. I could multiply instances of this condition of affairs, which permeates all grades of working people here. Even household servants are imbued with opposition to doing the slightest thing but what is strictly in line with their particular employment. It can readily be seen that the prevalence of this cast-iron, hard-and-fast custom adds enormously to the ultimate cost of labour, although the individual wages actually paid here are much lower than in America. Americans who have been inclined to come to England to establish factories have often been forced to abandon their intentions, because of the disadvantages they would be under by reason of the system above explained."

" I came here some little while ago to revive an old English business," writes the manager of a considerable undertaking in the Midlands to me. " I found that the owners had gone in the past on the principle of using very cheap labour and very poor machines. I tried to get them to put a little up-to-date machinery in. ' Why should we ? ' they replied. ' These machines have done our work all right for thirty years, and we do not see why we should go to the expense of changing now.' What can I do when hampered by such chiefs ? " Yet this business is one where up-to-date machinery is essential for success if it is in any.

Climate is a factor in competition which must not be ignored, and climate is against us. We take things easier than do men in the drier air of the North Atlantic States. Consequently it has been found time after time that the same output cannot be had here even with equally up-to-date machinery. As a case in point, a big English paper-making firm laid down an American machine, at a cost of £10,000, guaranteed to turn out 500 ft. of paper a minute. After a few weeks it was found that the average production was only about half this.

The buyers wrote complaining, whereupon the makers offered, if their English representative was given charge of the mill for thirty days, to raise the production to this point or take back the plant. The representative went down to the mill, rented a small house with a big garden, and took over command. In a few days he had won the liking of every man there. He effected some minor improvements, but no important change.

Then one evening he called the hands together. " Boys," said he, " your proprietor is coming down to-morrow. I want that day made a red-letter day in the history of this mill. Let us show him what we can turn out when we try. Then in the evening all of you come up to my grounds. There'll be tables out there, and chairs, and all the liquor you want."

The men entered into the spirit of the thing.

Next day they toiled as never before, and the new machine registered an output of 525 feet a minute. The English owner kept the machine, but the American frankly admitted that it was impossible to keep up the output here. Yet in a score of mills in America the same kind of machine is daily doing the maximum work.

The most unpromising factor in the situation to-day is the way Americans are preparing for the trades of to-morrow, while we are largely contenting ourselves with holding our own in older manufactures. In the electric industry the favourite excuse for our backwardness has been that no one could have foreseen the present enormous demand. Yet every man with eyes in his head saw it five years ago.

It requires little foresight to realize that very soon the trade in gas-engines will increase quite sixfold. To my knowledge, at least one American-English house is making careful preparation for this increase, and hopes to scoop the whole business when it comes. There is a German patent gas-engine which will also stand a good chance. But one hears no rumours of British firms preparing for this boom.

In the automobile trade America came in third, but is pushing ahead. France secured the cream of the trade, and has built up a great automobile industry ; Germany is working hard. In England speculators and company promoters took the matter up and after throwing away enormous sums disgusted the investing public. Now, while we are manufacturing on a comparatively small scale, American designers and manufacturers with costly plant and giant works are turning out in wholesale fashion cheap machines for the coming popular demand.

In electric automobilism, to which many look for the greatest future of this industry, the American is now easily first.   Month by month he is increasing the running capacity without recharging, and before long he will have on the market a victoria that can do from eighty to a hundred miles when once charged.

Then our present carriage makers will become patchers and repairers of the imported American machines.   And this is what is going on everywhere.   We are becoming the hewers of wood and drawers of water, while the most skilled, the most profitable, and the easiest trades are becoming American.

CHAPTER XXI

CAN WE MEET AMERICA?

WHAT attitude is England to adopt to the American industrial invasion? Are we to welcome it, and to regard the Americans as our allies in commerce, or are we to oppose it as a blow at our commercial position?

At the present time, when politicians are talking vaguely of invoking the aid of the law against our rivals, the question demands consideration. But a very little reflection will show that we cannot regard the invasion wholly as a good thing, or wholly as bad. In parts it inflicts heavy loss on our commerce. In parts it indisputably is to our benefit.

Take the benefits first. American labour-saving appliances, American manufactured goods, American food and American ideas have been the greatest aids to our industry. The American machine tool increases the capacity of our workshops. The twenty guineas spent on a Remington or Barlock typewriter enables the merchant to have better and faster work done in his office. The half-guinea spent by a writer on an American fountain pen yields much more than it costs. The housewife who buys an American carpet sweeper or an American baking dish benefits by the purchase.

American raw materials keep our factories employed. American food enables our work people to live in greater comfort at less expense than they otherwise could. Exclude American cotton, American corn and American meat, and there would be want and famine in our land in a month.

We gain, too, by the interchange of ideas, and by the adoption of American notions. American methods now being introduced to our factories profit us. The revolution in our iron works on American lines enables us the better to meet the world, and the quickening of our workmen by American contractors may help England to regain her place. The many factories built by American firms in this country are to-day supplying not only England but also a large part of the world outside of America with goods which otherwise would have come from the United States. One might name as an instance of this the Hoe Printing Machine Works, the Westinghouse Electrical Works, the McGuire Brake Factory, the premises the Kodak people have built at Harrow for manufacturing their supplies, and the works of Burroughs & Wellcome in Kent for manufacturing tabloids. This list is greatly growing, and the longer it grows the greater we benefit.

American ingenuity too is benefiting us by

solving the many problems that have long baffled our own people, and solving them to our profit. The activity of Mr. Yerkes in London transit is the most prominent instance of this. Who can doubt but that Mr. Yerkes in transforming London from one of the slowest to one of the best cities on earth for transit is making every Londoner his debtor? He may, it is true, enormously increase his own fortune in doing so, but he deserves to.

So far from opposing the introduction of American improvements, even to the profit of the Americans in this country, we should welcome them and aid them in every way. The pity is that we have not adopted them the more largely. We need a Wanamaker to come here to teach us how to modernize our Sunday Schools. We need to learn the American way of dealing with patents, and we will never fully enter into our own until we recognize as they do in America the principle of adequate pay for good work. We need a quickening up, and Americans are the people to do it for us. Doubtless if the conditions of the nineteenth century could have existed for ever we might have got along very comfortably. But as they could not, and as we would not without compulsion adapt ourselves to the newer state of affairs, it was as well the Americans should be the agents for our regeneration.

We have, it is true, to decide whether we are going to be a subordinate people, allowing the Americans to take the supreme rule of our industries,

R

or whether we are going to retain our old chieftainship. But we will not keep our place by any other method than that of raising our industrial conditions up to those of America. Only by improving the physical growth and mental development of our people, and by putting the best brains of our nation, unrestricted by old traditions, into our industrial concerns can we hope to advance. The time when the governing classes of this country treat commerce as a matter for lofty patronage and scornful misunderstanding must go by. To-day we are hindered in a hundred ways by inadequate and pernicious laws. We see industry after industry almost throttled by mere legislative stupidity. We find our traders refused the facilities which every other progressive government willingly gives its people. We witness commerce fostered in other lands, while in England it is severely left alone. Only recently there was a notorious case of one trade—Manilla fibre—which formerly had been almost solely in London hands, taken from our merchants and from London by the tariff regulations of America. Asked about it in Parliament, the representative of the Government knew nothing of the matter and denied that any such thing was taking place. Pulled up later by those acquainted with the facts, he sheltered himself behind a verbal quibble, to excuse the ignorance of his own department! When we show that we are in earnest, and that commerce which gives bread to our sons and work to our people is of at least as much importance to us a commercial nation as the minor politics of small states, only then shall we begin to recover lost ground. Will this day ever come? In the present state of public affairs, who knows?

The vague talk of a policy of commercial retaliation against America and of protection in answer to American protective laws loses its force when we remember one fact. Industrially, we cannot do without America; America can do without us, although only at heavy loss. This land is dependent on the outside world. America could shut the whole outside world out, and yet find, in her own borders, sufficiency. Doubtless the British Empire could do within itself what America can do for herself. But for the moment, whatever the immediate future may bring forth, we are not in the position to bring a united British Empire against a United States. Even if we were, it would require abundant proof to satisfy our people that we would benefit by doing so.

The purchase outright of British manufactories by Americans is a blow to our prestige. But in many instances the American purchasers settle in our midst, and become English in their turn. England has in the past showed great powers of absorbing outer peoples; in the future she will show the same. To build high barriers against America would be folly. If we wish to hold what America is taking from us we must do so by proving ourselves as good men as the Americans, as good in business energy, in education, in technical training, in working capacity, and in inventive skill. Then the competition of the two peoples will result in the world's benefit. And sore as Englishmen may be at the successes of their rivals, they have not yet forgotten that we are one kin, too closely knit together for trade disputes to sever.

AMERICAN BUSINESS ABROAD

Origins and Development
of the Multinational Corporation

An Arno Press Collection

Abrahams, Paul Philip. *The Foreign Expansion of American Finance and its Relationship to the Foreign Economic Policies of the United States, 1907-1921.* 1976

Adams, Frederick Upham. *Conquest of the Tropics:* The Story of the Creative Enterprises Conducted by the United Fruit Company. 1914

Arnold, Dean Alexander. *American Economic Enterprises in Korea, 1895-1939.* 1976

Bain, H. Foster and Thomas Thornton Read. *Ores and Industry in South America.* 1934

Brewster, Kingman, Jr. *Antitrust and American Business Abroad.* 1958

Callis, Helmut G. *Foreign Capital in Southeast Asia.* 1942

Crowther, Samuel. *The Romance and Rise of the American Tropics.* 1929

Davids, Jules. *American Political and Economic Penetration of Mexico, 1877-1920.* 1976

Davies, Robert Bruce. *Peacefully Working to Conquer the World:* Singer Sewing Machines in Foreign Markets, 1854-1920. 1976

de la Torre, Jose R., Jr. *Exports of Manufactured Goods from Developing Countries.* 1976

Dunn, Robert W. *American Foreign Investments.* 1926

Dunning, John H. *American Investment in British Manufacturing Industry.* 1958

Edelberg, Guillermo S. *The Procurement Practices of the Mexican Affiliates of Selected United States Automobile Firms.* 1976

Edwards, Corwin. *Economic and Political Aspects of International Cartels.* 1944

Elliott, William Yandell, Elizabeth S. May, J.W.F. Rowe, Alex Skelton, Donald H. Wallace. *International Control in the Non-Ferrous Metals.* 1937

Estimates of United States Direct Foreign Investment, 1929-1943 and 1947. 1976

Eysenbach, Mary Locke. *American Manufactured Exports, 1879-1914.* 1976

Gates, Theodore R., assisted by Fabian Linden. *Production Costs Here and Abroad.* 1958

Gordon, Wendell C. *The Expropriation of Foreign-Owned Property in Mexico.* 1941

Hufbauer, G. C. and F. M. Adler. *Overseas Manufacturing Investment and the Balance of Payments.* 1968

Lewis, Cleona, assisted by Karl T. Schlotterbeck. *America's Stake in International Investments.* 1938

McKenzie, F[red] A. *The American Invaders.* 1902

Moore, John Robert. *The Impact of Foreign Direct Investment on an Underdeveloped Economy: The Venezuelan Case.* 1976

National Planning Association. *The Creole Petroleum Corporation in Venezuela.* 1955

National Planning Association. *The Firestone Operations in Liberia.* 1956

National Planning Association. *The General Electric Company in Brazil.* 1961

National Planning Association. *Stanvac in Indonesia.* 1957

National Planning Association. *The United Fruit Company in Latin America.* 1958

Nordyke, James W. *International Finance and New York.* 1976

O'Connor, Harvey. *The Guggenheims.* 1937

Overlach, T[heodore] W. *Foreign Financial Control in China.* 1919

Pamphlets on American Business Abroad. 1976

Phelps, Clyde William. *The Foreign Expansion of American Banks.* 1927

Porter, Robert P. *Industrial Cuba.* 1899

Queen, George Sherman. *The United States and the Material Advance in Russia, 1881-1906.* 1976

Rippy, J. Fred. *The Capitalists and Colombia.* 1931

Southard, Frank A., Jr. *American Industry in Europe.* 1931

Staley, Eugene. *Raw Materials in Peace and War.* 1937

Statistics on American Business Abroad, 1950-1975. 1976

Stern, Siegfried. *The United States in International Banking.* 1952

U.S. Congress. House of Representatives. Committee on Foreign Affairs. *The Overseas Private Investment Corporation.* 1973

U.S. Congress. Senate. Special Committee Investigating Petroleum Resources. *American Petroleum Interests in Foreign Countries.* 1946

U.S. Dept. of Commerce. Office of Business Economics. *U.S. Business Investments in Foreign Countries.* 1960

U.S. Dept. of Commerce. Office of Business Economics. *U.S. Investments in the Latin American Economy.* [1957]

U.S. Dept. of Commerce and Labor. *Report of the Commissioner of Corporations on the Petroleum Industry:* Part III, Foreign Trade. 1909

U.S. Federal Trade Commission. *The International Petroleum Cartel.* 1952

Vanderlip, Frank A. *The American "Commercial Invasion" of Europe.* 1902

Winkler, Max. *Foreign Bonds, an Autopsy:* A Study of Defaults and Repudiations of Government Obligations. 1933

Yeoman, Wayne A. *Selection of Production Processes for the Manufacturing Subsidiaries of U.S.-Based Multinational Corporations.* 1976

Yudin, Elinor Barry. *Human Capital Migration, Direct Investment and the Transfer of Technology:* An Examination of Americans Privately Employed Overseas. 1976